Book A

Critical & Creative Thinking with Attribute Blocks

Bob Willcutt

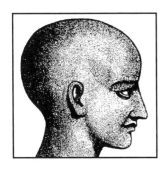

© 1998
CRITICAL THINKING BOOKS & SOFTWARE
www.criticalthinking.com
P.O. Box 448 • Pacific Grove • CA 93950-0448
Phone 800-458-4849 • FAX 408-393-3277
ISBN 0-89455-704-1
Printed in the United States of America

TABLE OF CONTENTS

INTRODUCTION

GENERAL INFORMATION

Critical and Creative Thinking with Attribute Blocks A (level K–2 ability) provides motivational block-pattern-building activities to develop critical thinking through logical reasoning and patterning. The book is divided into four types of activities: Matrices, Trains, Ring Challenges, and Mystery Blocks. The activities in this book, as well as those of Book B (grades 3–5 ability), are designed to lead student thinking from the simple and concrete to complex, abstract reasoning. The hands-on aspect of the block activities, especially at levels K–1, is critical. Students can develop their capacity for meaningful abstraction from the solid basis in pattern work with real blocks.

Matrices activities present row-and-column block arrangements whose shared attributes students must discover. Students learn to recognize an emerging pattern in the matrix and then fill in the "holes" to complete it by classifying blocks based on color, size, and shape.

In Trains, students recognize and complete linear patterns to form "trains" of blocks. Patterns become as complex as student readiness allows.

In Ring Challenges, students classify in order to add blocks to a labelled ring. They must also determine the class(es) of rings based on blocks already inside a given ring. To determine the appropriate label for a set of blocks, students learn efficient questioning strategy—they learn that the choice of which block to check (i.e., Does the large blue square belong?) makes a difference in meeting the challenge quickly.

The questioning activities of Mystery Blocks help students learn the importance of questioning strategy. They ask yes-no questions in order to receive clues, one at a time (i.e., the mystery block is *not* blue; the mystery block *is* large…). From the given clues, students continually refine their sorting of the blocks (possible mystery blocks vs. not possible mystery blocks) until the one mystery block is exposed.

Through their experiences with all the block activities, students learn an overriding concept in pattern evolution. In the early stage of pattern building, there is an openness, or flexibility, so that the pattern may take on several forms. The student has a choice in how that pattern will "come out." At some point, however, the pattern becomes fixed so that there are no options left; the builder must complete the pattern in a specified way, for the outcome is predetermined.

TEACHING SUGGESTIONS

Use as much of the material as is appropriate for your students. For example, Kindergartners might do only the first level of each section.

For early learners, it is important that students use real blocks, whether activities are done with the whole class, with a small group, or individually. Instead of doing all activities with the whole group, you may model one activity, following the dialogue given, and provide other activities, of the same type, as small-group or individual exercises led by an aide.

At the top of each activity page are directions to the teacher. Oral directions to the students are in bold text. The numbered activity shows how the blocks should be set up for the student (color is designated by the letter on each block). Assessments may be used to check whether the student has mastered the skills for each level before proceeding to the next.

Depending on student readiness, the leader may either set up the blocks as shown on the activity page or have the student reproduce the arrangement. The leader should explain the exercise in terms familiar to the student and have the student complete it, verbalizing as necessary (i.e., "This block goes here because we need a big red one then a small red one…," etc.).

Developmentally advanced students may be ready to deal with a little abstraction. Initial modeling, instruction, and group participation should still focus on real blocks; however, older students may be able to move, after some experience with real blocks, from concrete to abstract work. (You may even let students with necessary motor skills complete an activity page by drawing shapes or filling in blanks). Only you, as their teacher, know the types of activities for which your students are ready.

MATERIALS NEEDED

From the Book

Activity and assessment worksheets are to be used as reference sheets for whole-class, small-group, or individual activities; these activities are to be led the same way as the modeling sessions given at the start of each level. (If you have students who could benefit by pencil/paper activities, you may copy the pages for student use.)

Matrices

Levels 1 & 2: Twenty-four attribute blocks (four shapes, three colors, two sizes).

Level 3: Thirty attribute blocks (five shapes, three colors, two sizes).

Trains

Level 1: Twenty-four attribute blocks (four shapes, three colors, two sizes).

Level 2: Thirty attribute blocks (five shapes, three colors, two sizes).

Ring Challenges

Level 1: Twenty-four attribute blocks (four shapes, three colors, two sizes). Enough yarn (*not* red, blue, or yellow) to make several large circles for enclosing sets of blocks; *nine* index cards, each labelled with one attribute: large, small, red, blue, yellow, circle, square, triangle, rectangle.

Level 2: Thirty attribute blocks (five shapes, three colors, two sizes). Enough yarn (*not* red, blue, or yellow) to make several large circles for enclosing sets of blocks; *ten* index cards, each labelled with one attribute: large, small, red, blue, yellow, circle, square, triangle, rectangle, hexagon.

Mystery Blocks

Level 1: Twenty-four attribute blocks (four shapes, three colors, two sizes).

Level 2: Thirty attribute blocks (five shapes, three colors, two sizes).

Attribute Blocks Used in this Book

24-Block Set

30-Block Set (adds hexagons)

Key: B = blue, R = red, Y = yellow

MATRICES LEVEL 1

Modeling Activity

PREPARATION

You will need a set of twenty-four attribute blocks: four shapes, three colors, and two sizes (shown on page iv). Gather all twenty-four blocks and put them in a non-transparent bag. Use a bag that will allow you to shake the blocks so all can hear them, but not see them.

Have the students seated in a circle with a large open space in the middle. With young children, you may want to mark each child's personal home base with a piece of tape.

In the center of the space, you will start building a matrix. A pre-marked grid will make the matrix easier to see (a square-tiled floor works well; otherwise you may want to mark a grid with tape).

Review the following lesson example before leading the students. Teacher dialogue is given in boldface type; substitute the names of your students and the chosen blocks as appropriate.

LESSON

It is worthwhile to explore the ways in which sound can reveal the nature of the contents of the bag. Shake the bag of blocks as you challenge students as follows:

What do you think I have in the bag? What are they made of? How many are there? Are they the same size? What can you tell by just listening to the noise they make? What sounds do they make?

Student responses to sound can prove very enlightening. Many students will relate the sound of the blocks to the sounds of cans, toys, etc. and identify the plastic construction of the blocks. Explore a few of their answers.

Students will next pull blocks out of the bag, and you will be placing them according to the finished matrix shown later.

Okay. Now I want to find out what is in the bag. We will go around the circle and, when it is your turn, you may put your hand in the bag, feel the contents of the bag, and then, when you are ready, take one item from the bag. You may not look into the bag. When you choose one item, you may show it to all of the class and we will try to decide what else may still be in the bag.

The first student draws [a large red square].

Good. What did you find, [Jennifer]? What can we call it?

Naturally, all the blocks are three-dimensional objects (cylinders, triangular prisms, rectangular solids, etc.), but you should use their two-dimensional surface names throughout these activities. The three-dimensional terminology would only be confusing at this time.

Okay. It is a [red square]. Let's put it here on the floor where everyone can see it.

Find the chosen block in the matrix below, and place it similarly, relative to the boundaries of your floor space. (You will now have only one block in your "matrix.")

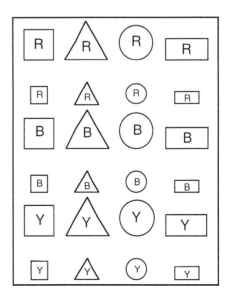

The next student draws [a large blue triangle.]

Okay. What is the name of this block? Yes. It is a [blue triangle]. Let's put it with the [red square].

Place the block in your "matrix" and choose the next student.

See if you can find something different from the first two blocks. Take your time.

The student pulls out [a small red circle].

Good. What is the name of this block?

[A red circle!]

Yes. It is [a red circle]...

You must continue until you have enough blocks to create a skeleton framework for the larger, final matrix (the minimum number needed will vary with student groups). Arrange the blocks in a skeleton matrix format as they are placed on the floor. After seven blocks are drawn and placed, you may (as an example) have the following arrangement:

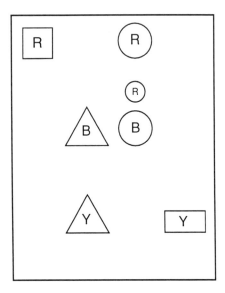

Have students continue to draw from the bag and place blocks until there is enough of a matrix to give students the information to predict what is left in the bag.

It is worthwhile to have students predict the blocks remaining in the bag as early as possible. It is perfectly okay for a prediction to be wrong (i.e., a *green* block or a *hexagon* or a duplicate block.) All predictions should be applauded, for we are dealing with probability and there is no way to be sure at this point.

Now I have a challenge for you. Without looking or touching, can you describe a block that may still be in the bag? Look at the blocks we have here on the floor. What do you think may still be in the bag? Listen. I will shake the bag again. Are there quite a few blocks still in the bag?

(Yes!)

Choose the next student in the circle...

Can you guess a block that may still be in the bag?

(The student guesses [a large yellow circle].)

Ah, yes. I think I do have [a large yellow circle] in the bag. Here it is. Will you place it on the floor where you think it belongs? How did you know I had a large yellow circle in the bag?

Continue having students guess and place blocks until they begin to see the solutions easily.

I will continue to go around the circle until we have identified all the blocks in the bag.

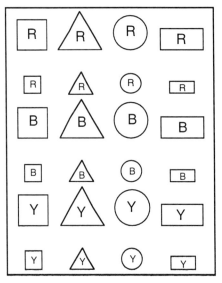

When the matrix is complete, you should introduce the word *matrix* and discuss visible patterns:

Now, look at all the blocks here in their correct places on the floor. They are arranged in *rows*, going side to side, and *columns*, going up and down. We call this arrangement of blocks in rows and columns a *matrix*.

How many squares do we have in our matrix? (6) How many triangles? (6) ...circles? (6) ...rectangles? (6) How many blocks do we have in all? (24)

How many red blocks do we have? (8) ...yellow blocks? (8) ...blue blocks? (8) How many blocks do we have altogether? (24)

How many large blocks do we have? (12) How many small blocks? (12) How many blocks do we have in all? (24)

Look at the blocks in the matrix and tell me one pattern you see. Can you see others?

Continue until students have identified several patterns in the matrix (i.e., large-small/large-small; square-triangle-circle-rectangle/square-triangle-circle-rectangle, etc.).

Calling each block by its correct attributes is an important contribution to the future work with attribute blocks. The order of the attributes is not important, but the correct three attribute values are essential.

I want to make sure we agree on the exact name for each block. Each block's name has exactly three parts, just as many of ours do. Each block has a shape name, a color name, and a size name. When it is your turn, give me the exact name for the block I pick up from the matrix.

After students have had a chance to name blocks, you can reinforce the correct names by hiding blocks and having students identify those that are missing. While students are not looking, remove a single block or as many as four. (Removing more than four blocks begins to defeat the purpose of using the patterns in the matrix to find the missing block.)

I am going to continue going around the circle, but this time, when it is your turn, I want you to cover your eyes. I will then take one or more blocks away from the design and put them back into the bag. When I tell you to look, you can tell me the exact name of each block I have removed and we will return the blocks to the matrix.

Give everyone a chance to name blocks.

Now you will rearrange the matrix while students look away, and they will then "fix the matrix." Students find this highly motivational and rewarding—everyone wants her/his own chance to fix the matrix!

Now I want you all to look out the window [or close your eyes]. While you are not looking, I am going to make some changes in the matrix.

Exchange several blocks so that the matrix is inconsistent.

Now you may look again. The matrix needs to be fixed! Who will come forward and fix the matrix for us?

Have a student set the matrix right.

Look, it is back the way it should be. Now, look out the window again. This time I will make it tougher.

It is important to allow each student to correct the matrix in her/his own way, and you will observe different learning styles evolving. It is also important that you, the leader, do *not* make too many changes in the original matrix or you will destroy the basic pattern.

Some students may make so many changes that they end up creating a new matrix. That's okay—the purpose is not to restore the original matrix, but to end with a consistent matrix.

Continue the session until all students have had a chance to fix the matrix.

LEVEL 1-Activities

Teacher: Using the 24-block set, arrange the matrix shown, then give oral directions (shown in bold). Blanks may be used to record student responses.

1 a.   **Look for a pattern in the matrix. How many blocks are missing? What are their names?**

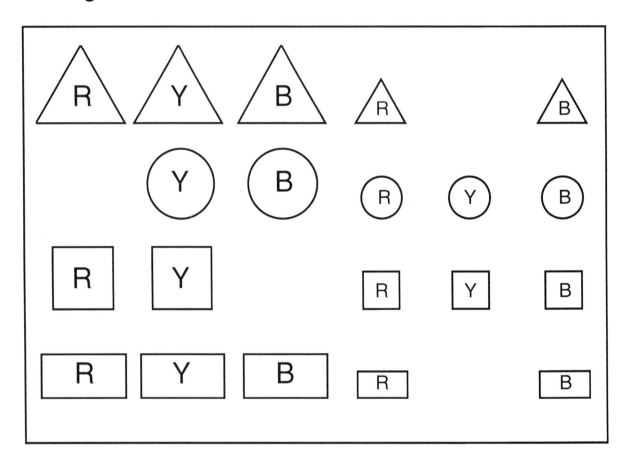

Number of missing blocks _____

Names of missing blocks _____

_____

LEVEL 1-Activities

Teacher: Using the 24-block set, arrange the matrix shown, then give oral directions (shown in bold). Blanks may be used to record student responses.

1 b.   Look for a pattern in the matrix. How many blocks are missing? What are their names?

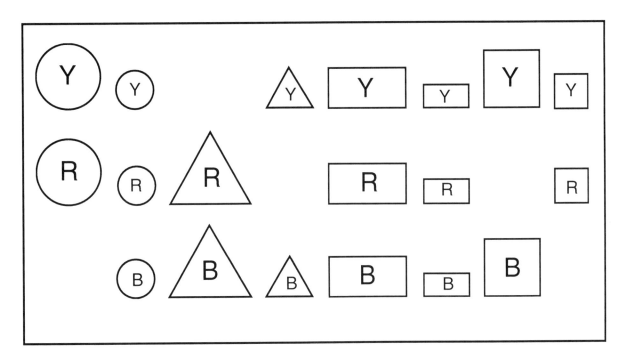

Number of missing blocks _____

Names of missing blocks _____

_____

LEVEL 1-Activities

Teacher: Using the 24-block set, arrange the matrix shown, then give oral directions (shown in bold). Blanks may be used to record student responses.

1 c.   **Look for a pattern in the matrix. How many blocks are missing? What are their names?**

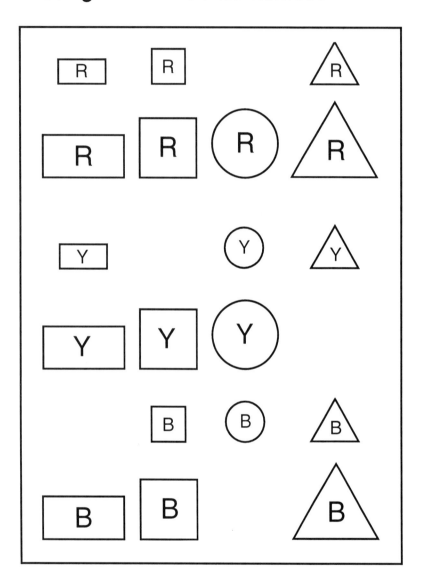

Number of missing blocks _____

Names of missing blocks _____

_____

LEVEL 1-Activities

Teacher: Using the 24-block set, arrange the matrix shown, then give oral directions (shown in bold). Blanks may be used to record student responses.

1d.   Look for a pattern in the matrix. How many blocks are missing? What are their names?

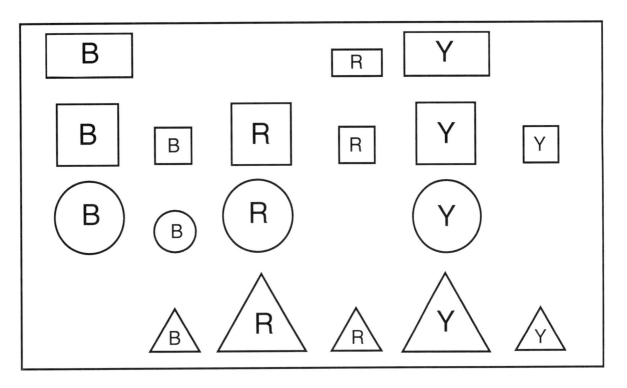

Number of missing blocks _____

Names of missing blocks _____

_____

LEVEL 1-Activities

Teacher: Using the 24-block set, arrange the matrix shown, then give oral directions (shown in bold). Blanks may be used to record student responses.

2 a.   Fix the matrix so it keeps a pattern.

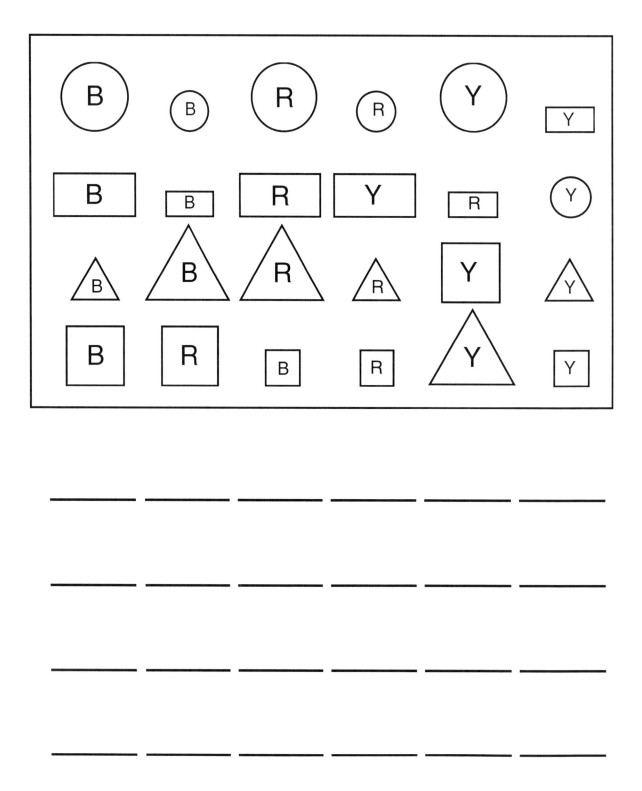

© 1998 Critical Thinking Books & Software · www.criticalthinking.com · 800-458-4849

LEVEL 1-Activities

Teacher: Using the 24-block set, arrange the matrix shown, then give oral directions (shown in bold). Blanks may be used to record student responses.

2 b. Fix the matrix so it keeps a pattern.

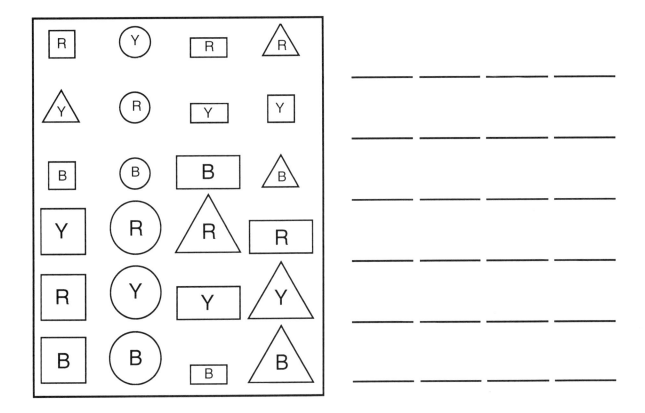

LEVEL 1-Activities

Teacher: Using the 24-block set, arrange the matrix shown, then give oral directions (shown in bold). Blanks may be used to record student responses.

2 c.   Fix the matrix so it keeps a pattern.

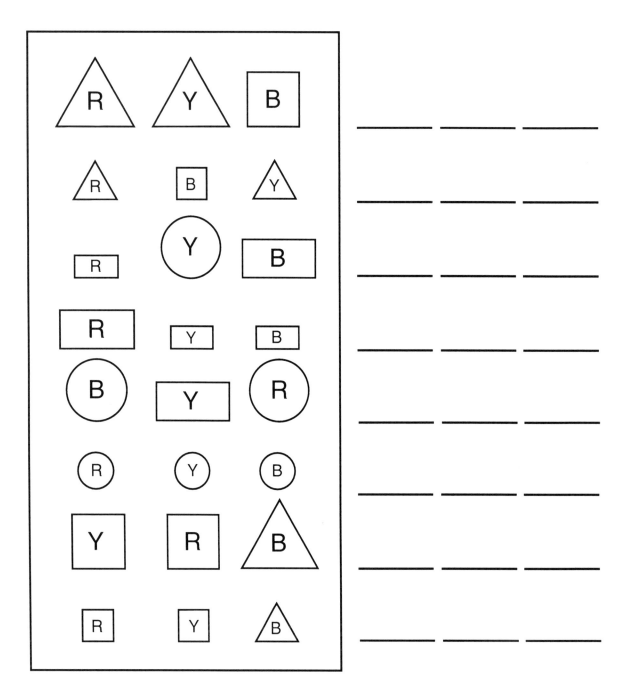

LEVEL 1-Activities

Teacher: Using the 24-block set, arrange the matrix shown, then give oral directions (shown in bold). Blanks may be used to record student responses.

2 d.   Fix the matrix so it keeps a pattern.

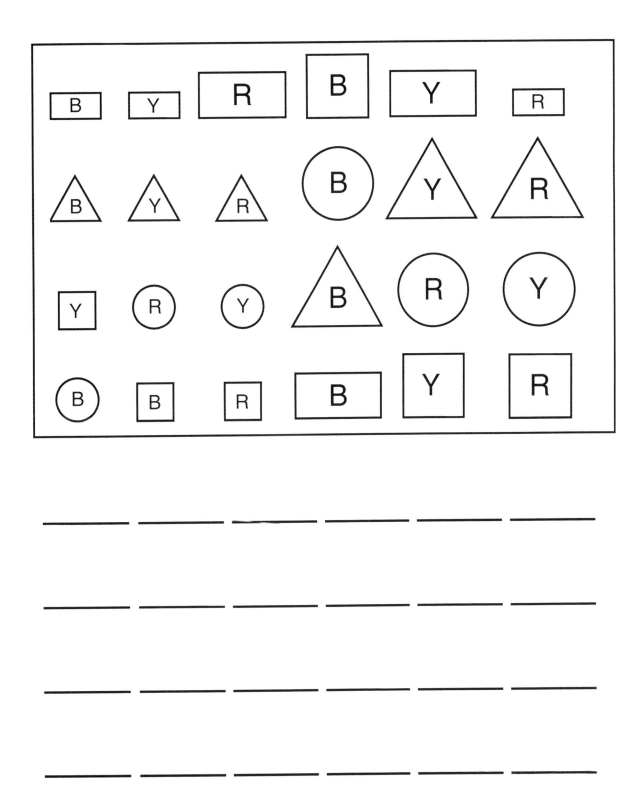

_____   _____   _____   _____   _____   _____

_____   _____   _____   _____   _____   _____

_____   _____   _____   _____   _____   _____

_____   _____   _____   _____   _____   _____

LEVEL 1-Assessments

Teacher: Using the 24-block set, arrange the matrix shown, then give oral directions (shown in bold). Blanks may be used to record student responses.

1 a.   **Look for a pattern in the matrix. How many blocks are missing? What are their names?**

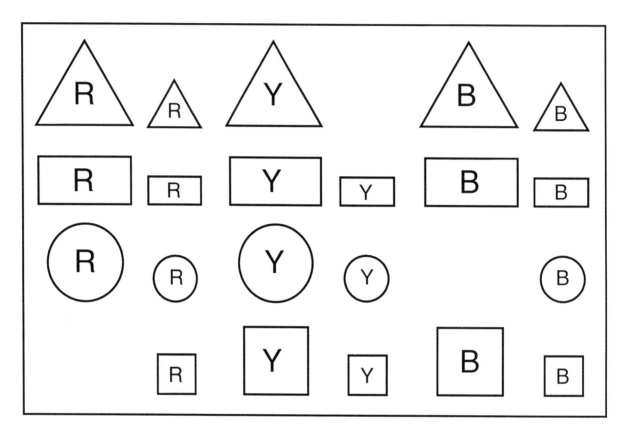

Number of missing blocks _____

Names of missing blocks _____

_____

LEVEL 1-Assessments

Teacher: Using the 24-block set, arrange the matrix shown, then give oral directions (shown in bold). Blanks may be used to record student responses.

1b. **Look for a pattern in the matrix. How many blocks are missing? What are their names?**

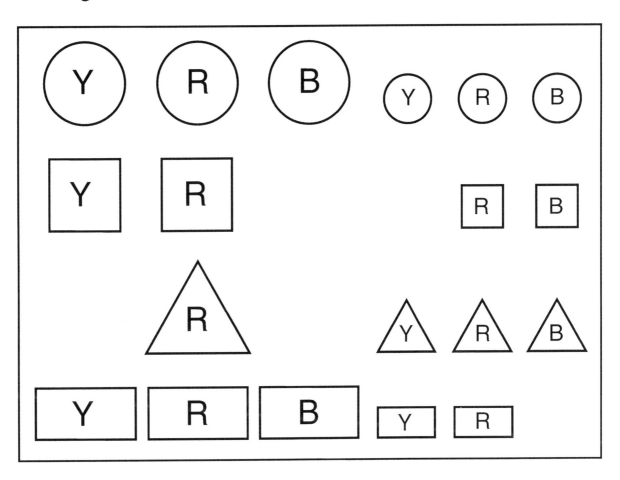

Number of missing blocks _____

Names of missing blocks _____

_____

LEVEL 1-Assessments

Teacher: Using the 24-block set, arrange the matrix shown, then give oral directions (shown in bold). Blanks may be used to record student responses.

2 a.   Fix the matrix so it keeps a pattern.

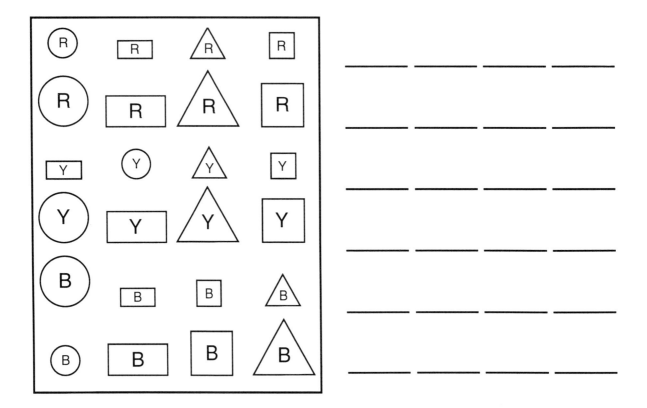

_____ _____ _____ _____

_____ _____ _____ _____

_____ _____ _____ _____

_____ _____ _____ _____

_____ _____ _____ _____

_____ _____ _____ _____

LEVEL 1-Assessments

Teacher: Using the 24-block set, arrange the matrix shown, then give oral directions (shown in bold). Blanks may be used to record student responses.

2 b.   Fix the matrix so it keeps a pattern.

_____   _____   _____   _____   _____   _____

_____   _____   _____   _____   _____   _____

_____   _____   _____   _____   _____   _____

_____   _____   _____   _____   _____   _____

MATRICES LEVEL 2
Modeling Activity

PREPARATION

You will need a set of 24 attribute blocks.

Have students seated in a circle with a large open space in the middle. The set of 24 blocks should be in the open space, to one side. In the center of the space, you will start building a matrix.

A pre-marked grid will make the matrix easier to see (a square-tiled floor works well; otherwise you may want to mark a grid with tape).

LESSON

We will use our set of twenty-four attribute blocks again today. They are all here in this space on the floor. Now, over here I am going to start building a matrix. This matrix will have six rows and four columns. I will put this large red rectangle here in one corner; it cannot be moved. Under it I will put the small yellow rectangle and then under it the large blue rectangle... (continue describing your actions as you place the blocks as shown below).

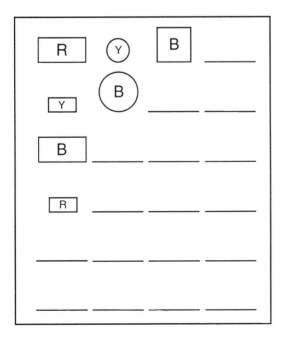

Now these seven blocks are in place; I have a certain matrix in my mind, and I wonder if you can come up and finish it. As I go around the circle, you may "pass" or you may come up and place one block in the matrix. If you are correct, the block stays; if not, the block goes back to the original pile. Remember, I have a set matrix in my mind. There may be other possible answers, but I am looking only for my matrix.

Have students continue adding to the matrix until it is complete, as shown below.

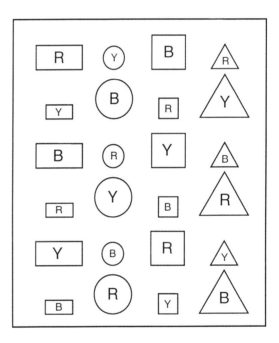

Good. Now you have done it. Tell me one pattern that you see. Another one... another one.... How many different patterns can we find?

At this point, you may begin a block "take away" activity, as in Level 1. Level 2 "take away" is more difficult as the matrix patterns are more complex.

Okay. Whose turn is it? Good. Close your

eyes [Erik]. Now I will take one or more blocks from the matrix and hide them. Open your eyes, [Erik]. What did I take?

Continue taking away blocks as students take turns guessing (replace the block after each correct guess) until all have had a chance.

Now you may start the "fix-it" activity. As in Level 1, do not make too many changes to the matrix or the basic patterns will become too difficult to see.

Now everyone look [out the window].

Change a few blocks by switching their places.

Okay. I have made some changes in the matrix. Who can fix the matrix?

Have students take turns until all have fixed the matrix.

LEVEL 2-Activities

Teacher: Using the 24-block set, arrange the matrix shown, then give oral directions (shown in bold). Blanks may be used to record student responses.

1 a. **Look for a pattern in the matrix. How many blocks are missing? What are their names?**

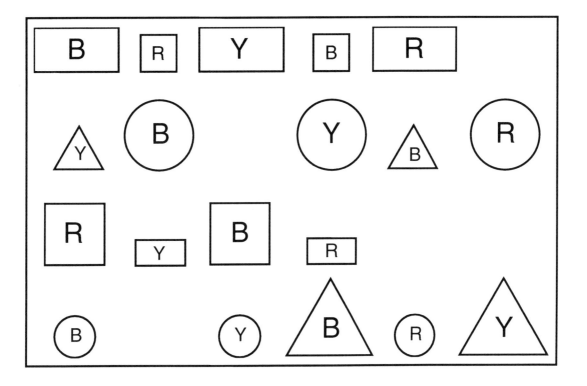

Number of missing blocks _____

Names of missing blocks _____

_____

_____

_____

LEVEL 2-Activities

Teacher: Using the 24-block set, arrange the matrix shown, then give oral directions (shown in bold). Blanks may be used to record student responses.

1b.   Look for a pattern in the matrix. How many blocks are missing? What are their names?

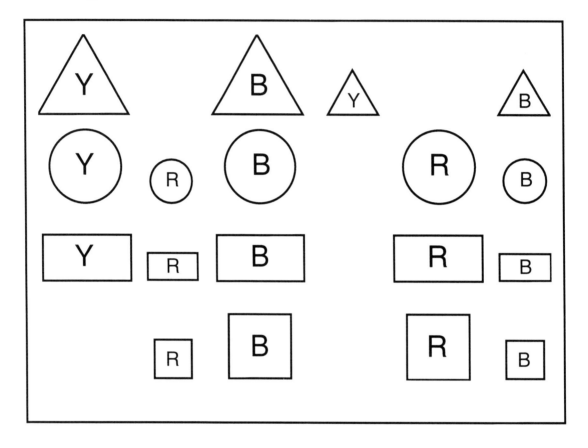

Number of missing blocks _____

Names of missing blocks _____

_____

_____

_____

LEVEL 2-Activities

Teacher: Using the 24-block set, arrange the matrix shown, then give oral directions (shown in bold). Blanks may be used to record student responses.

Look for a pattern in the matrix. How many blocks are missing? What are their names?

1 c.

R	Y
B Y R B	
R B Y R	
B Y	
B Y B	
R B Y	

Number of missing blocks

_____

Names of missing blocks

_____

_____

_____

_____

d.

R R B	
R B	
Y Y R R	
Y	
R	
B B Y	
B Y Y	

Number of missing blocks

_____

Names of missing blocks

_____

_____

_____

_____

LEVEL 2–Activities

Teacher: Using the 24-block set, arrange the matrix shown, then give oral directions (shown in bold). Blanks may be used to record student responses.

2 a.   Fix the matrix so it keeps a pattern.

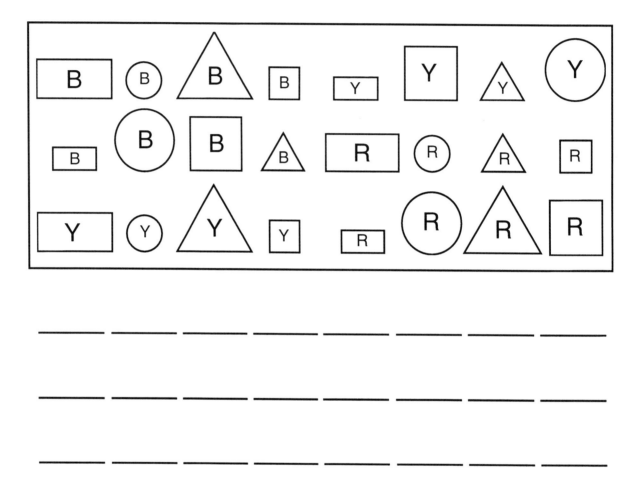

_____ _____ _____ _____ _____ _____ _____ _____

_____ _____ _____ _____ _____ _____ _____ _____

_____ _____ _____ _____ _____ _____ _____ _____

LEVEL 2-Activities

Teacher: Using the 24-block set, arrange the matrix shown, then give oral directions (shown in bold). Blanks may be used to record student responses.

2 b.   Fix the matrix so it keeps a pattern.

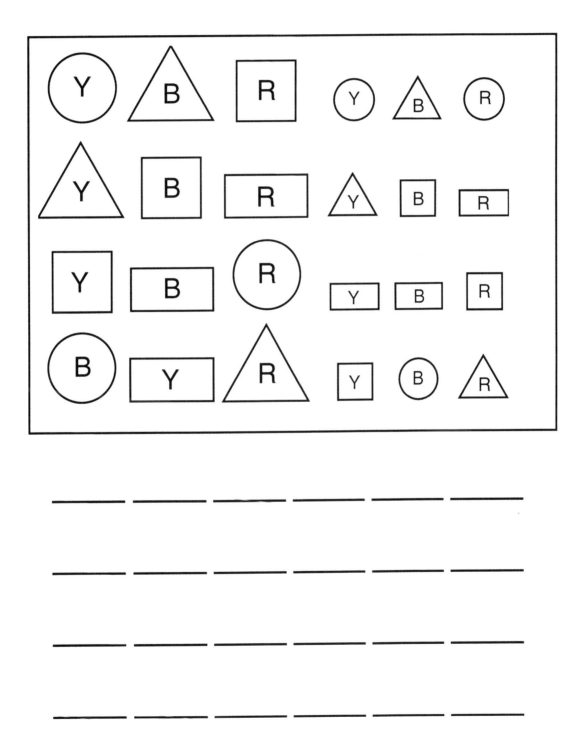

—— —— —— —— —— ——

—— —— —— —— —— ——

—— —— —— —— —— ——

—— —— —— —— —— ——

LEVEL 2-Activities

Teacher: Using the 24-block set, arrange the matrix shown, then give oral directions (shown in bold). Blanks may be used to record student responses.

Continue the pattern to finish the matrix.

3 a.

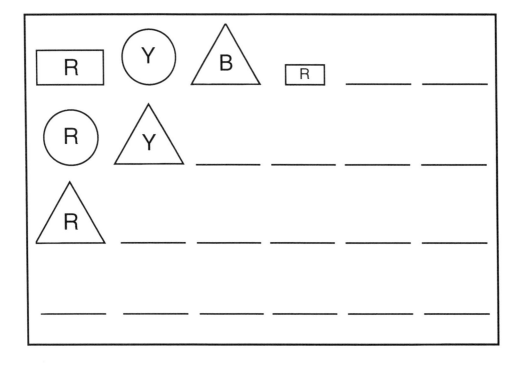

b.

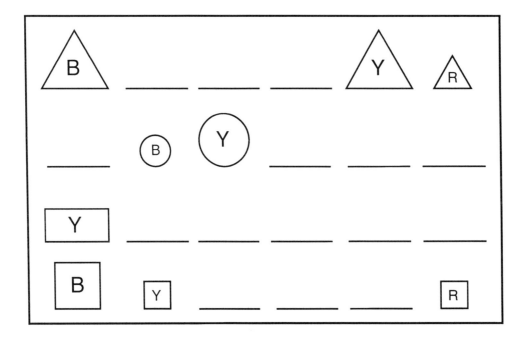

LEVEL 2-Activities

Teacher: Using the 24-block set, arrange the matrix shown, then give oral directions (shown in bold). Blanks may be used to record student responses.

3 c.   Continue the pattern to finish the matrix.

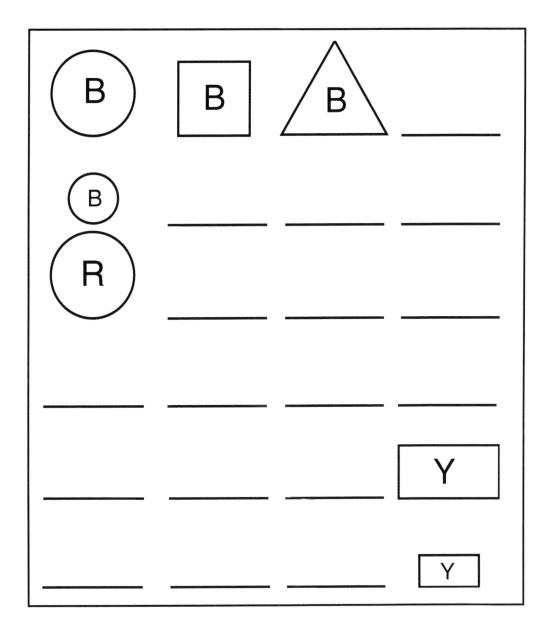

LEVEL 2-Activities

Teacher: Using the 24-block set, arrange the matrix shown, then give oral directions (shown in bold). Blanks may be used to record student responses.

3 d. Continue the pattern to finish the matrix.

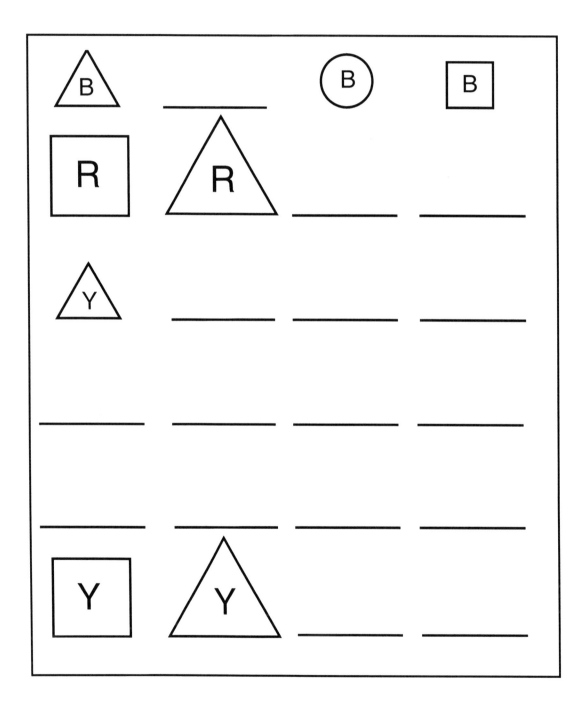

LEVEL 2-Activities

Teacher: Using the 24-block set, arrange the matrix shown, then give oral directions (shown in bold). Blanks may be used to record student responses.

3 e.   Continue the pattern to finish the matrix.

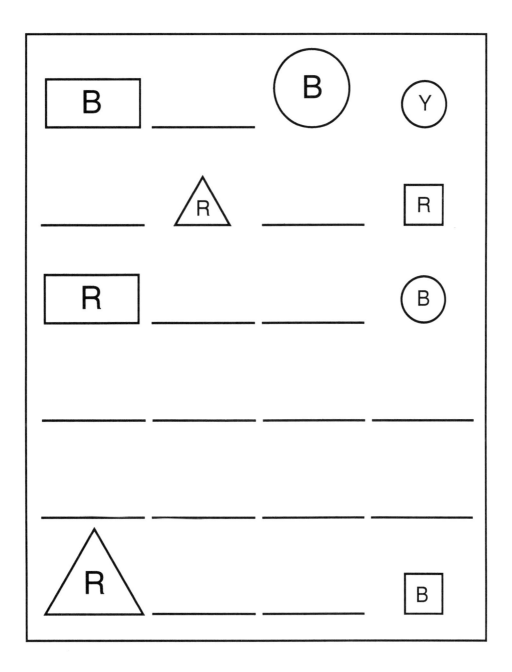

LEVEL 2-Activities

Teacher: Using the 24-block set, arrange the matrix shown, then give oral directions (shown in bold). Blanks may be used to record student responses.

3 f.   Continue the pattern to finish the matrix.

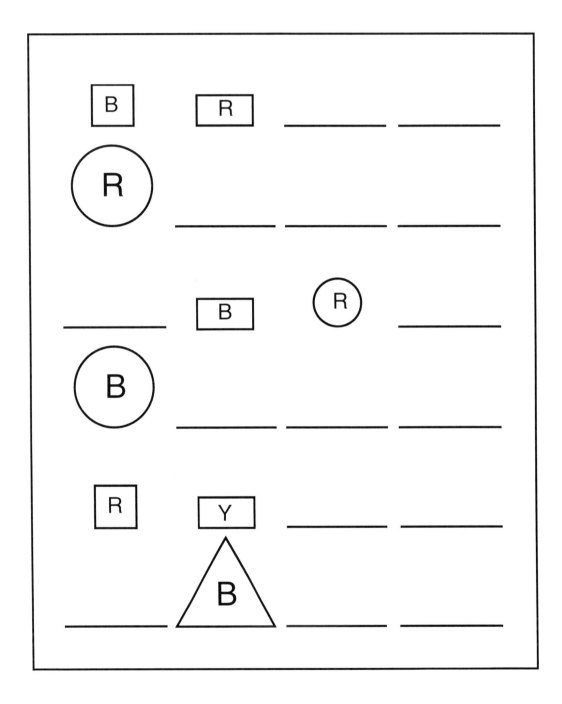

LEVEL 2-Activities

Teacher: Using the 24-block set, arrange the matrix shown, then give oral directions (shown in bold). Blanks may be used to record student responses.

3 g.   Continue the pattern to finish the matrix.

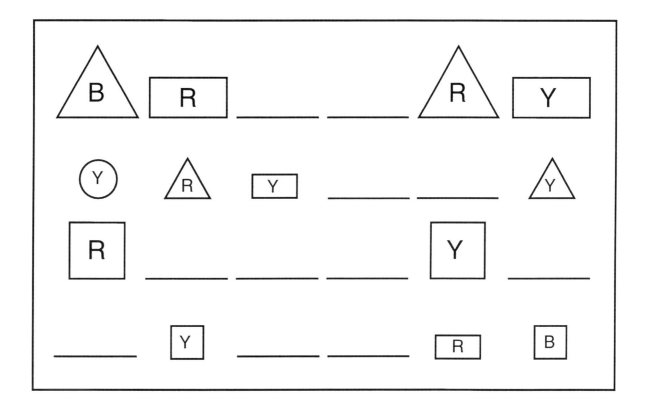

LEVEL 2-Activities

Teacher: Using the 24-block set, arrange the matrix shown, then give oral directions (shown in bold). Blanks may be used to record student responses.

3 h. Continue the pattern to finish the matrix.

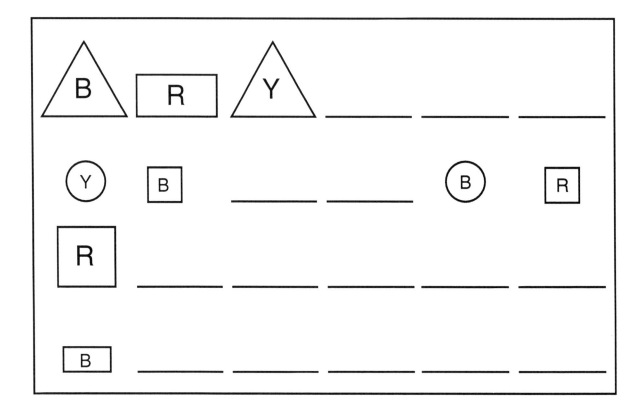

LEVEL 2-Assessments

Students find the pattern in the matrix, then give the number of blocks that are missing and the name of each. Blanks may be used to record their responses.

1. **Look for a pattern in the matrix. How many blocks are missing? What are their names?**

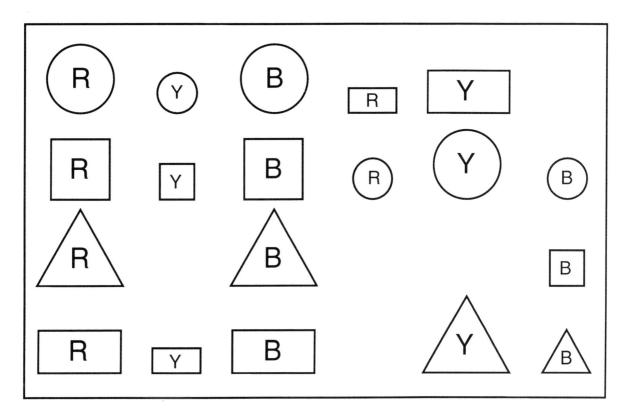

Number of missing blocks _____

Names of missing blocks _____

_____

_____

_____

LEVEL 2-Assessments

Students fix the matrix so it has a consistent pattern. Blanks may be used to record their responses.

2.   **Fix the matrix so it keeps a pattern.**

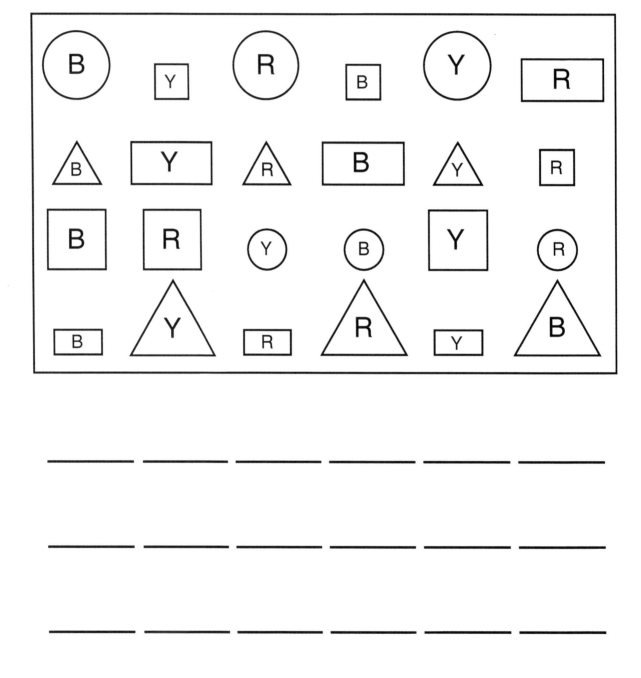

_____   _____   _____   _____   _____   _____

_____   _____   _____   _____   _____   _____

_____   _____   _____   _____   _____   _____

_____   _____   _____   _____   _____   _____

LEVEL 2-Assessments

Teacher: Using the 24-block set, arrange the matrix shown, then give oral directions (shown in bold). Blanks may be used to record student responses.

3 a.   Continue the pattern to finish the matrix.

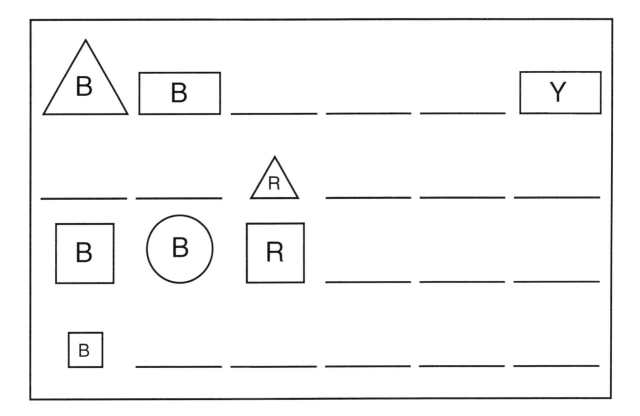

LEVEL 2-Assessments

Teacher: Using the 24-block set, arrange the matrix shown, then give oral directions (shown in bold). Blanks may be used to record student responses.

3 b.   Continue the pattern to finish the matrix.

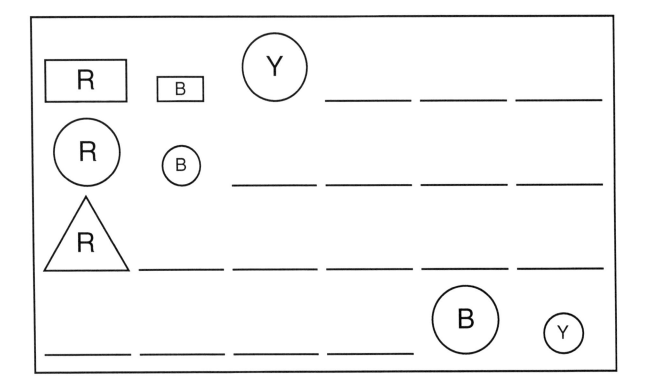

LEVEL 2-Assessments

Teacher: Using the 24-block set, arrange the matrix shown, then give oral directions (shown in bold). Blanks may be used to record student responses.

3 c.   Continue the pattern to finish the matrix.

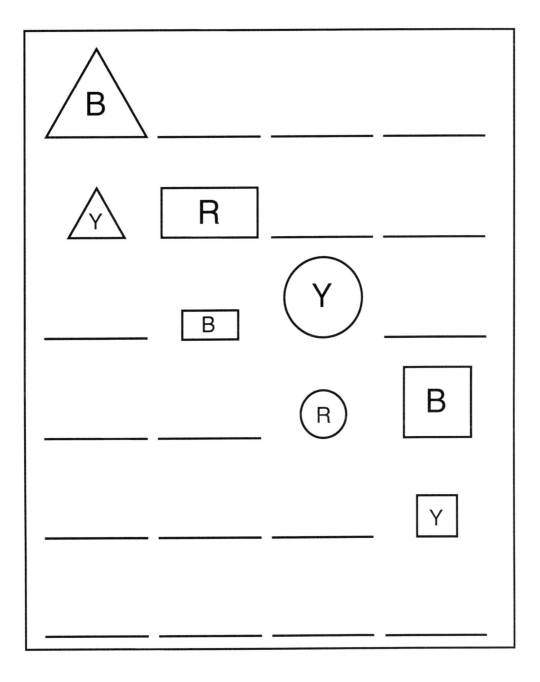

LEVEL 2-Assessments

Teacher: Using the 24-block set, arrange the matrix shown, then give oral directions (shown in bold). Blanks may be used to record student responses.

3 d.   Continue the pattern to finish the matrix.

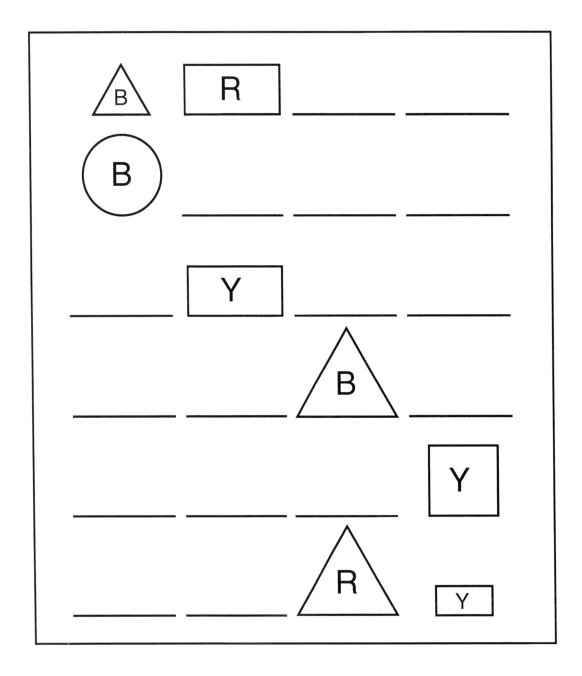

MATRICES LEVEL 3
Modeling Activity

PREPARATION

You will need a set of thirty attribute blocks: five shapes, three colors, and two sizes.

Have students seated in a circle with a large open space in the middle. The set of thirty blocks should be in the open space, to one side. In the center of the space, you will start a 5 x 6 matrix.

A pre-marked grid will make the matrix easier to see (a square-tiled floor works well; otherwise you may want to mark a grid with tape).

LESSON

With the students gathered around the space, begin the lesson as follows:

We will use this set of *thirty* attribute blocks today. They are all here in this space on the floor. Now, over here I am going to start building a matrix. This matrix will have six rows and five columns. I will put this large blue hexagon here in the corner; it cannot be moved. Under it I will put the small yellow hexagon and then under it the large red hexagon ... (con-tinue describing your actions as you place the blocks, as shown below).

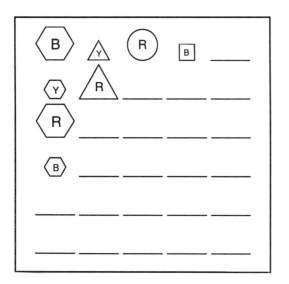

Now these eight blocks are in place and cannot be moved; I have a certain matrix in my mind, and I wonder if you can come up and finish it. As I go around the circle, you may pass or you may come up and place one block in the matrix. If you are correct, the block stays; if not, the block goes back to the original pile. Remember, I have a set matrix in my mind. There may be other possible answers, but I am looking only for *my* matrix.

Proceed around the circle, having students place blocks in the matrix until it is finished as follows:

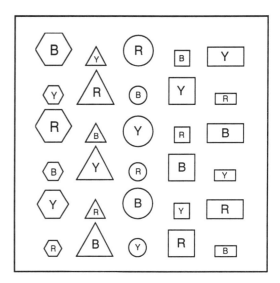

Fine. The matrix is finished; it is the one I had in my mind. Tell me one pattern that you see... another one... another... How many different patterns can we find?

The "take away" and "fix-it" activities discussed in Levels 1 and 2 can be included next. Both of these activities can be very difficult if too many blocks are removed or too many blocks are switched in the "fix-it" activity. Restrict changes to four or five blocks.

While students are not looking, remove a single block or as many as four.

(Removing more than four blocks begins to defeat the purpose of using the patterns in the matrix to find the missing block.)

I am going to continue going around the circle, but this time, when it is your turn, I want you to cover your eyes. I will then take one or more blocks away from the design and put them back into the bag. When I tell you to look, you can tell me the exact name of each block I have removed and we will return the blocks to the matrix.

"Fixing the matrix" has proven to be highly motivational and rewarding for students. There seems to be something very special about getting the matrix right that is very satisfying for all, and every student wants her/his own chance to fix the matrix.

It is important to allow each student to correct the matrix in her/his own way, and it is interesting to observe the different learning styles that will evolve. It is also important not to make too many changes in the original matrix or you will destroy the basic pattern.

Some students may make too many changes and end up creating a new matrix. This is okay; the purpose is not to restore the original matrix but rather to end with a consistent matrix.

Now I want you all to look out the window [or close your eyes]. While you are not looking, I am going to make some changes in the matrix.

Move blocks so that the matrix is inconsistent.

Now you may look again. The matrix needs to be fixed! Who will come forward and fix the matrix for us?

The student sets the matrix right.

Look, it is back the way it should be. Look out the window again. This time I will make it tougher.

Continue until all students have had a chance to fix the matrix.

LEVEL 3-Activities

Teacher: Using the 30-block set, arrange the matrix shown, then give oral directions (shown in bold). Blanks may be used to record student responses.

1 a.   Look for a pattern in the matrix. How many blocks are missing? What are their names?

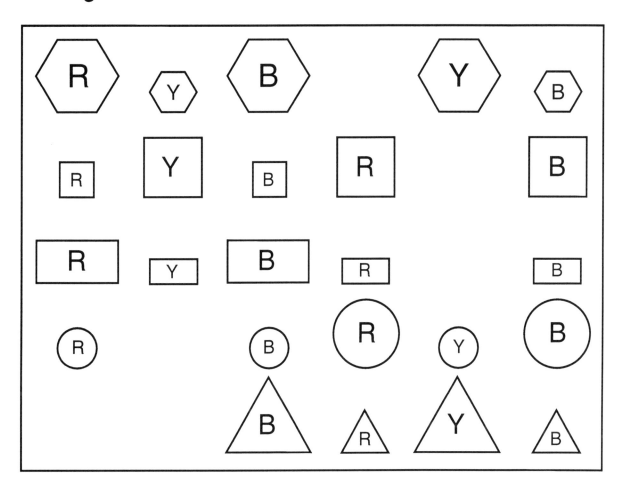

Number of missing blocks _____

Names of missing blocks _____

_____

_____

_____

LEVEL 3-Activities

Teacher: Using the 30-block set, arrange the matrix shown, then give oral directions (shown in bold). Blanks may be used to record student responses.

1 b.   Look for a pattern in the matrix. How many blocks are missing? What are their names?

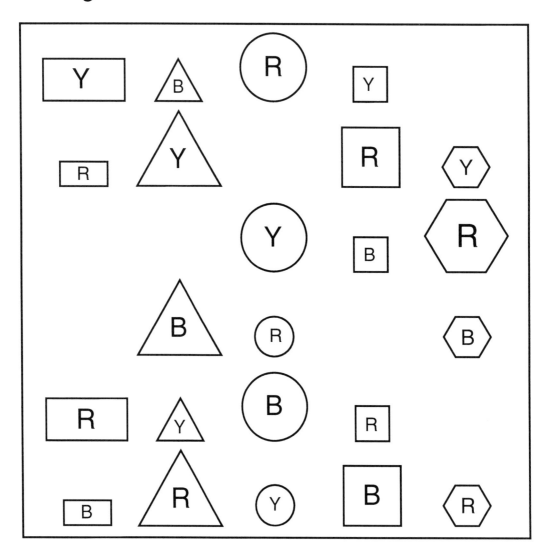

Number of missing blocks _____

Names of missing blocks _____

_____

_____

_____

LEVEL 3-Activities

Teacher: Using the 30-block set, arrange the matrix shown, then give oral directions (shown in bold). Blanks may be used to record student responses.

1c.   **Look for a pattern in the matrix. How many blocks are missing? What are their names?**

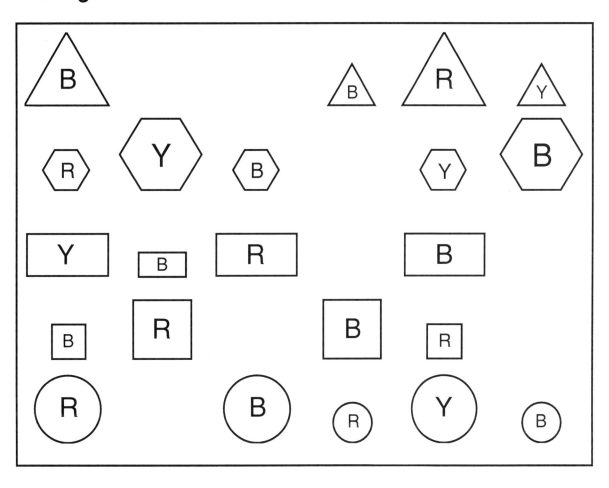

Number of missing blocks _____

Names of missing blocks _____

_____

_____

_____

LEVEL 3-Activities

Teacher: Using the 30-block set, arrange the matrix shown, then give oral directions (shown in bold). Blanks may be used to record student responses.

1d. Look for a pattern in the matrix. How many blocks are missing? What are their names?

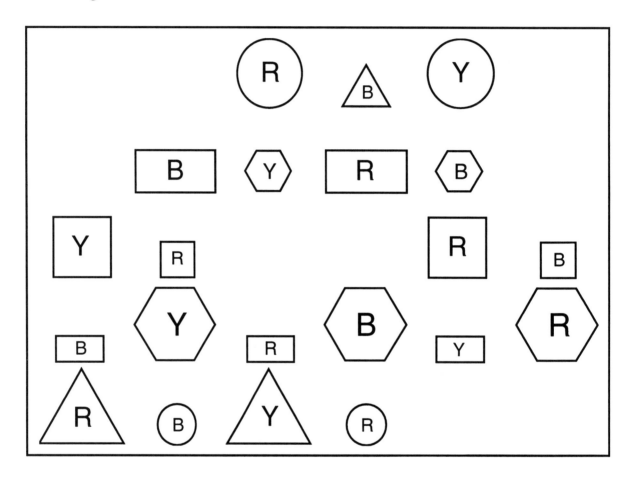

Number of missing blocks _____

Names of missing blocks _____

_____

_____

_____

LEVEL 3-Activities

Teacher: Using the 30-block set, arrange the matrix shown, then give oral directions (shown in bold). Blanks may be used to record student responses.

2 a.   Fix the matrix so it keeps a pattern.

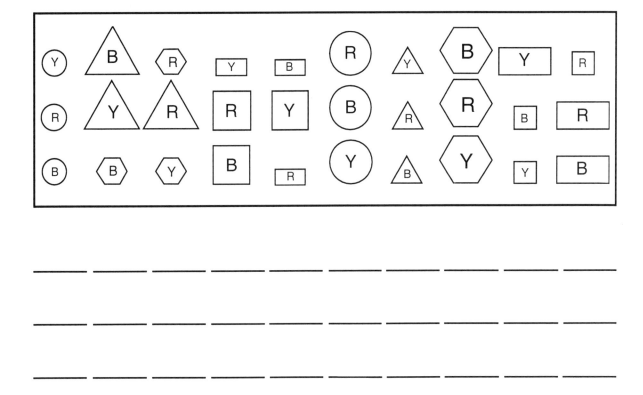

___ ___ ___ ___ ___ ___ ___ ___ ___ ___

___ ___ ___ ___ ___ ___ ___ ___ ___ ___

___ ___ ___ ___ ___ ___ ___ ___ ___ ___

LEVEL 3-Activities

Teacher: Using the 30-block set, arrange the matrix shown, then give oral directions (shown in bold). Blanks may be used to record student responses.

2 b.   Fix the matrix so it keeps a pattern.

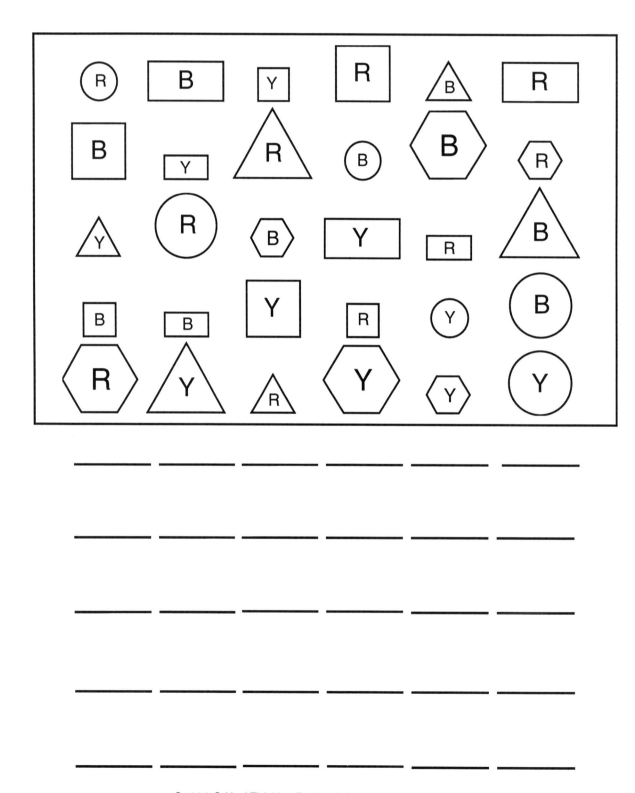

_____ _____ _____ _____ _____ _____

_____ _____ _____ _____ _____ _____

_____ _____ _____ _____ _____ _____

_____ _____ _____ _____ _____ _____

_____ _____ _____ _____ _____ _____

LEVEL 3-Activities

Teacher: Using the 30-block set, arrange the matrix shown, then give oral directions (shown in bold). Blanks may be used to record student responses.

Continue the pattern to finish the matrix.

3 a.

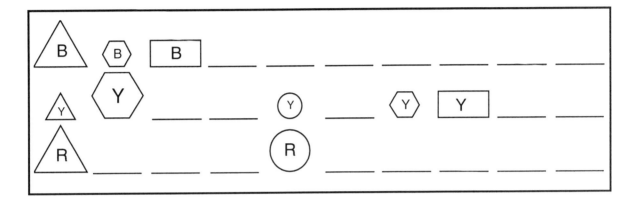

b.

LEVEL 3-Activities

Teacher: Using the 30-block set, arrange the matrix shown, then give oral directions (shown in bold). Blanks may be used to record student responses.

3 c.   Continue the pattern to finish the matrix.

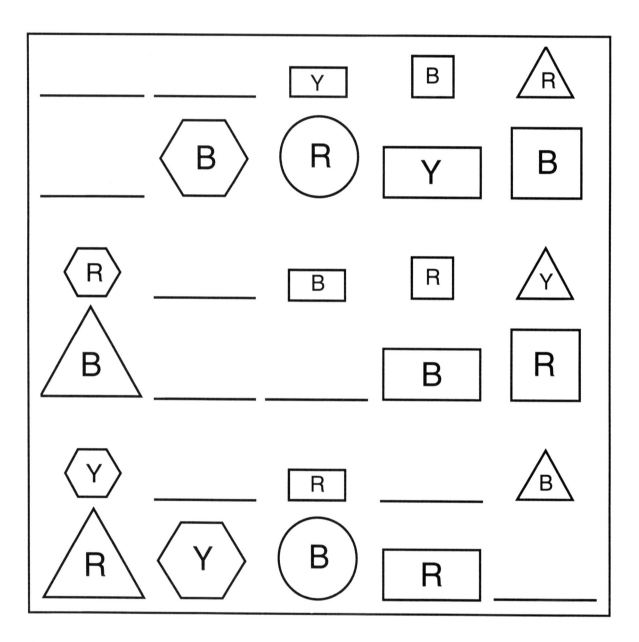

LEVEL 3-Activities

Teacher: Using the 30-block set, arrange the matrix shown, then give oral directions (shown in bold). Blanks may be used to record student responses.

3 d. Continue the pattern to finish the matrix.

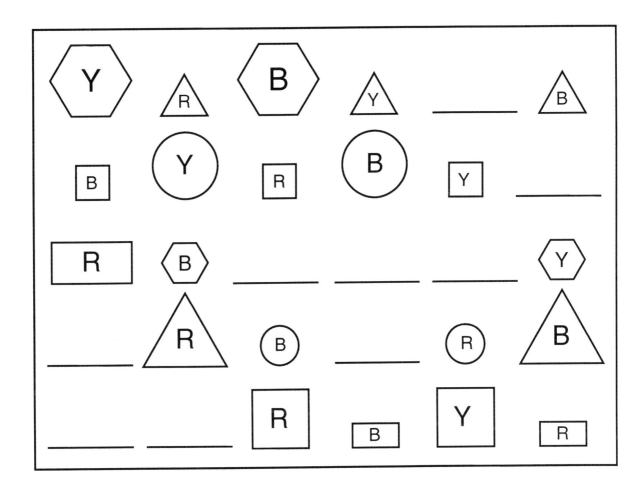

LEVEL 3-Activities

Teacher: Using the 30-block set, arrange the matrix shown, then give oral directions (shown in bold). Blanks may be used to record student responses.

3 e.   Continue the pattern to finish the matrix.

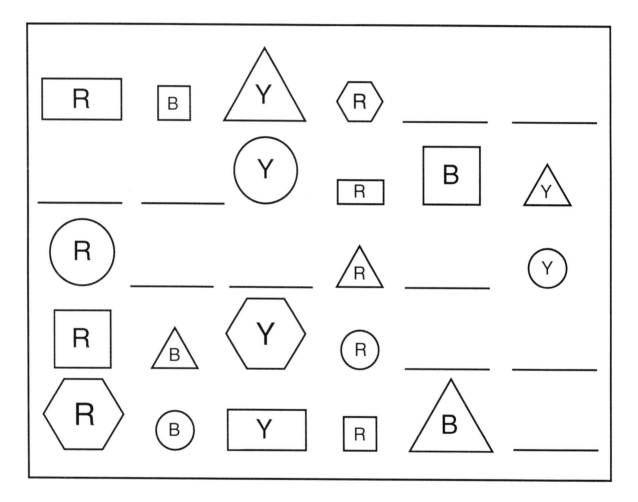

LEVEL 3-Activities

Teacher: Using the 30-block set, arrange the matrix shown, then give oral directions (shown in bold). Blanks may be used to record student responses.

3 f.   Continue the pattern to finish the matrix.

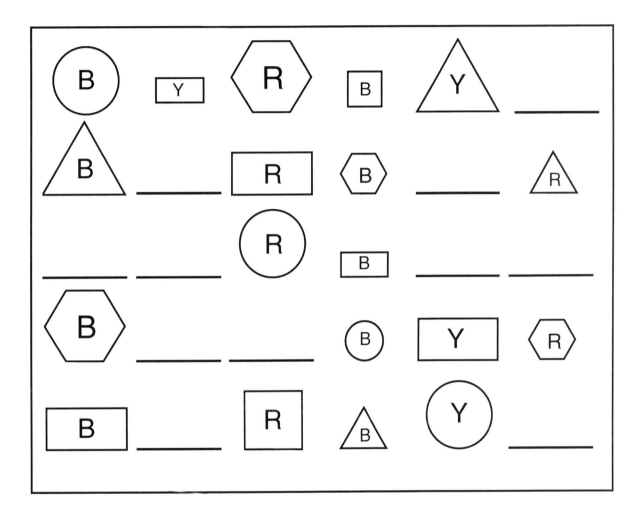

LEVEL 3-Activities

Teacher: Using the 30-block set, arrange the matrix shown, then give oral directions (shown in bold). Blanks may be used to record student responses.

Continue the pattern to finish the matrix.

3 g.

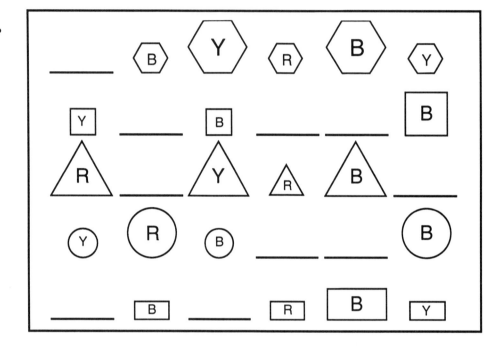

h.

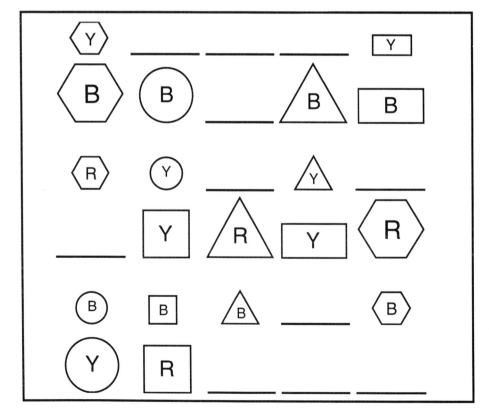

LEVEL 3-Assessments

Teacher: Using the 30-block set, arrange the matrix shown, then give oral directions (shown in bold). Blanks may be used to record student responses.

1.   **Look for a pattern in the matrix. How many blocks are missing? What are their names?**

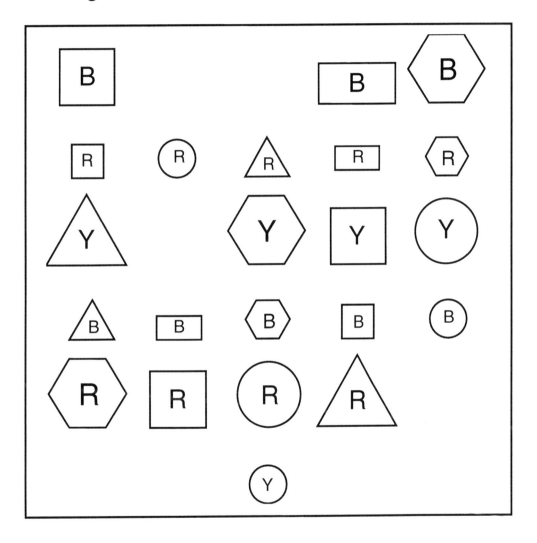

Number of missing blocks _____

Names of missing blocks _____

_____

_____

_____

LEVEL 3-Assessments

Teacher: Using the 30-block set, arrange the matrix shown, then give oral directions (shown in bold). Blanks may be used to record student responses.

2.   Fix the matrix so it keeps the pattern.

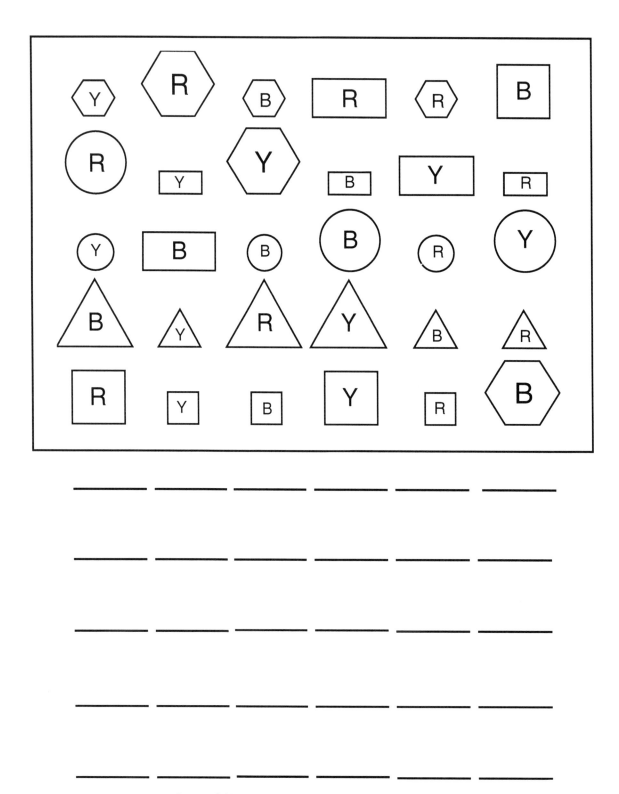

_____ _____ _____ _____ _____ _____

_____ _____ _____ _____ _____ _____

_____ _____ _____ _____ _____ _____

_____ _____ _____ _____ _____ _____

_____ _____ _____ _____ _____ _____

LEVEL 3-Assessments

Teacher: Using the 30-block set, arrange the matrix shown, then give oral directions (shown in bold). Blanks may be used to record student responses.

3 a.   Continue the pattern to finish the matrix.

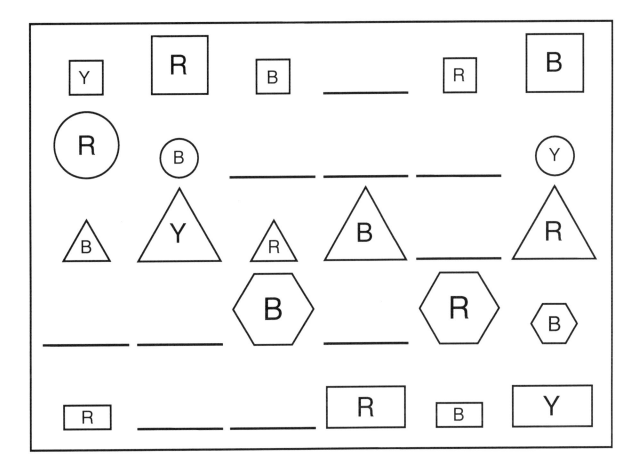

LEVEL 3-Assessments

Teacher: Using the 30-block set, arrange the matrix shown, then give oral directions (shown in bold). Blanks may be used to record student responses.

Continue the pattern to finish the matrix.

3 b.

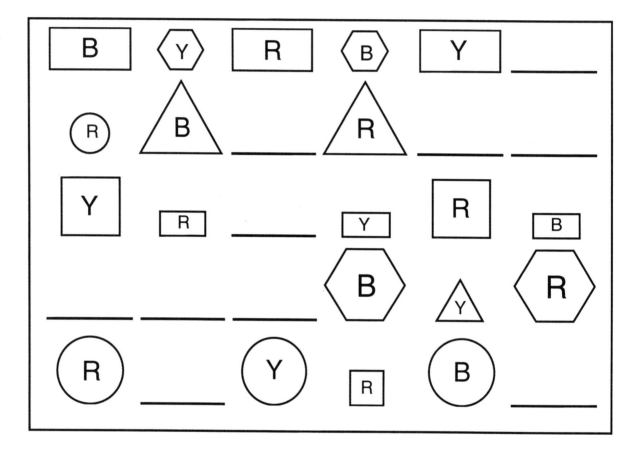

c.

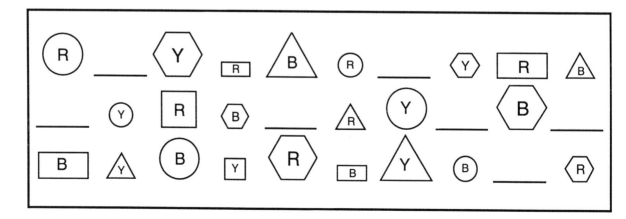

LEVEL 3-Assessments

Teacher: Using the 30-block set, arrange the matrix shown, then give oral directions (shown in bold). Blanks may be used to record student responses.

3 d.   Continue the pattern to finish the matrix.

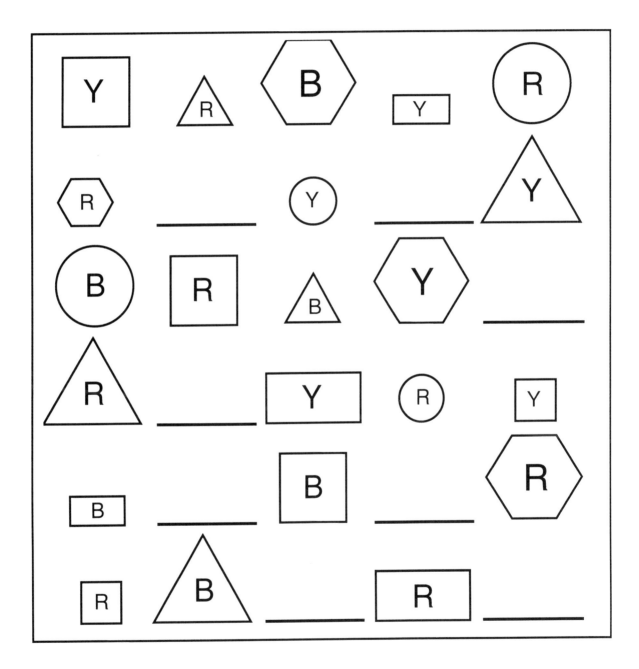

TRAINS LEVEL 1

Modeling Activity

PREPARATION

You will need a set of twenty-four attribute blocks: four shapes, three colors, and two sizes.

Have the students seated in a circle with a large open space in the middle. With young children, you may want to mark each child's personal home base with a piece of tape.

In the center of the space, you will start a pattern "train" of blocks and place as many cars as required for the students to recognize the emerging pattern.

It is important that the students understand that the leader has a particular train (pattern) in mind and the group is trying to build that train. Students may see other patterns, and those can be discussed, but to start with we are looking for one definite train. Later, you will encourage students to create their own trains following a logical pattern, but that creativity will be more productive after experiencing a few set patterns.

A possible beginning train sequence:

Review the following lesson example before leading the students. Teacher dialogue is given in boldface type; substitute the names of your students and the chosen blocks as appropriate.

LESSON

Start laying pieces for the train as you describe your actions:

I am going to start making a long train. Here is the engine and here is the first car. Now I will add another car. And now here is another car. Can you see what car I will add next?

This is how we will continue to build our train. I will go around the circle and ask you if you would like to add a car to the train. If you

want to try, fine. If not, that is fine too. I will tell you if the block you choose is the block I am looking for to keep the train going.

When all have had a chance to add to the train, proceed as follows:

Let's change the rules a little. When it is your turn, you may continue to add a car to the train until you make a mistake. If you make a mistake, then you must return to your seat and give the next student a chance.

Let students take turns, each adding cars until a mistake is made. Students of all ages seem to find this an exciting challenge. It also allows you to assess your students easily, as you can tell quickly when a student has found the pattern or when the student doesn't see the pattern.

After the train is complete, encourage students to comment on what they see.

Wonderful! Look at our train. What do you see? Can you tell us one pattern you see as you look at our train? Does somebody else see another pattern?

The discussion can be rich with pattern observations, some of which may be on the "original side." Younger students may see a collection of passenger cars, cattle cars, mail cars, oil tanker cars, etc. As long as the observation follows a logical pattern, it is acceptable.

Now, you will take away one, two, or even three blocks to give students the challenge of using the overall train pattern to help identify the missing pieces:

Okay, [Jose], I want you to close your eyes. I am going to take away one car from the train. Now, I want you to open your eyes. What block or car did I take?

After the student answers [i.e., The big blue square!], repeat the challenge for each student so all have the chance to describe a missing block.

Now students are ready for the "fix the train" activity, which offers another way for them to establish the finished pattern:

Now I want you all to close your eyes. While you have your eyes closed, I am going to change part of the train.

Exchange two of the blocks.

Now, open your eyes. [Andrea], will you come here and fix the train? I want it to be correct again.

Students seem to get an extra degree of satisfaction by making the train right, or whole again, and this can be an important event for them to experience. In altering the train, do not change more than three or four cars or the original pattern may become lost. In fixing a train, a student may totally alter the train from its original orientation. This is not wrong if the finished product follows a definite pattern. You may want to let students know this as you increase the number of blocks:

Now, [Geraldo], will you come here and fix the train? I want it to be correct again. It doesn't have to look _exactly_ like it did before, but it must have a complete pattern.

Continue until all have had a chance to fix the train. Then, you may repeat the train-building activities with another pattern:

I think I will take this train apart and start a new train. Here is my new engine, my first car, my second car…

Continue describing your actions as before in building the new train.

The six trains in the activities that follow incorporate the most basic patterns. (It is a good idea to master this level of work before moving on to "one-difference," "two-difference," and "three-difference" types of trains in _Attribute Blocks_ Book B.) It should be noted that there is some degree of flexibility in these basic trains. For example, in the first train, there will be a choice of shapes after the circles are completed. Triangles or squares can come next, so this train does not have a unique solution. The same kind of situation will occur in the third train.

LEVEL 1-Activities

Teacher: For each activity, arrange the partial train as shown and give oral directions (shown in bold). Responses may be recorded on the lines.

Finish building the train so that it uses all 24 blocks and keeps the pattern.

1.

_____

_____

2.

_____

_____

3.

_____

_____

LEVEL 1-Activities

Teacher: For each activity, arrange the partial train as shown and give oral directions (shown in bold). Responses may be recorded on the lines.

Finish building the train so that it uses all 24 blocks and keeps the pattern.

4.

5.

6.

LEVEL 1-Assessments

Teacher: For each activity, arrange the partial train as shown, and give oral directions (shown in bold). Blanks may be used for student responses.

Add three more cars to the train, keeping the pattern.

1. (B) (B) △B △B ☐B ☐B ☐B ☐B (Y) ___ ___ ___

2. [R] [Y] [B] [R] [Y] [B] △R △Y ___ ___ ___

3. △Y [Y] (Y) [Y] △Y [Y] (Y) [Y] △B [B] ___ ___ ___

4. [B] [B] [R] [R] ___ [Y] (B) ___ (R) (R) (Y) (Y) ___ △B △R △R

LEVEL 1-Assessments

Teacher: Arrange the partial train as shown, and give oral directions (shown in bold). Blanks may be used to record student responses.

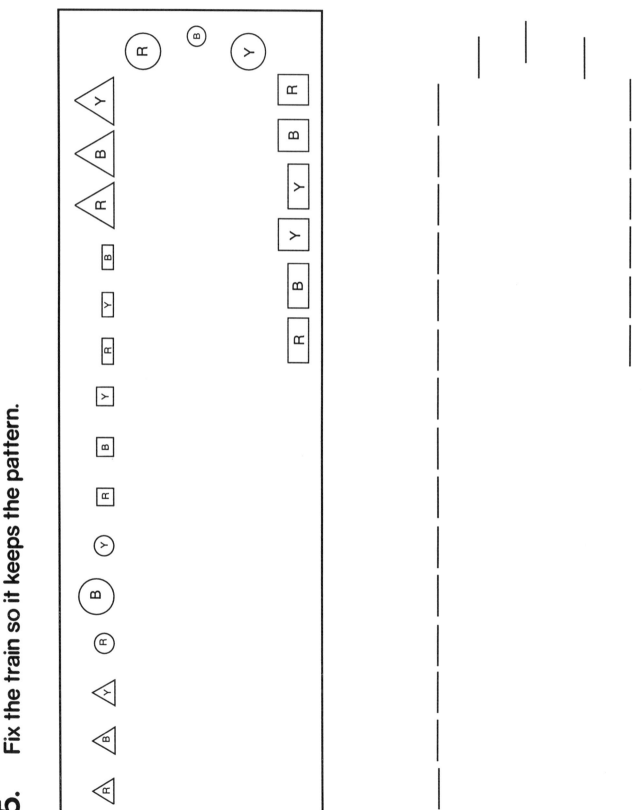

5. Fix the train so it keeps the pattern.

TRAINS LEVEL 2

Modeling Activity

PREPARATION

You will need a set of twenty-four attribute blocks: four shapes, three colors, and two sizes.

Have students seated in a circle with a large open space in the middle. In the center of the space, you will start a pattern "train" of blocks and place as many cars as required for the students to recognize the emerging pattern.

The patterns for this level follow logical color/shape/size arrangements. Most of the first nine activities have unique answers—a definite pattern has been established in each case. Activities 2 and 8, however, are flexible. For example, in Activity 2 there is a shape choice: either circles or rectangles may be used after the six squares.

In the modeling activity, you will give enough blocks of the train to indicate a possible pattern but not so many that the pattern is obvious. It should be clear that the group is to make one *particular* train that follows the leader's pattern. Other patterns are possible, but we are looking for one definite pattern at this time. The example below uses the pattern given in activity 1:

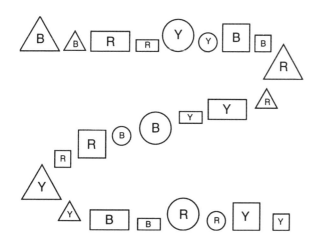

LESSON

Start laying pieces for the train as you describe your actions:

I will start making a train that will use all of the 24 blocks. Here is the engine, the first car, the second car, and the third car. The train I have in my mind follows a particular pattern. I will go around the circle and ask you if you would like to add a car to the train. If you would like to try, fine. If not, that's fine too. If your train car fits my pattern, you may continue to add cars until you choose a wrong car. Once you take your hand off the block, it's an official "try" and you must leave the block.

Students continue building the train, one car at a time, until it is complete. Encourage students to analyze the patterns of the train:

Good. What patterns do you see in our train? Tell me one pattern that you see.

Discuss a few patterns that the students notice (i.e., alternating sizes, alternating colors). To reinforce the overall train pattern, proceed with the "take-away" activity below, in which you remove up to three or four blocks and hide them:

[Yolanda], will you please close your eyes? Good. Now, while you have your eyes closed, I am going to take some blocks away from our finished train. Okay, open your eyes. Give me the exact names for each of the blocks that I have taken.

Students should give you the three distinguishing characteristics of each block (i.e., "big blue triangle"). Continue the activity until students have shown, by their answers, that they see the pattern and can accurately describe a missing component.

At this point, the following "fix the train" activity can be a powerful learning and motivating activity. You will change a few blocks while the students are not looking, then they must recognize the "mistake" and rearrange the blocks correctly:

Now, I want everyone to look [out the big window]. While you are not watching, I am going to change a few cars in our train.

Make the change.

Okay. Now look back at our train. [Pito], will you come up and fix our train?

By now, students should be comfortable enough with the pattern so that you may start changing the overall shape of the train. You will begin to build patterns in a circular format, beginning with activity 10 (shown below).

I wonder if we can make a circular train. This will be a train in which the caboose will fit correctly with the engine. That means our last piece will fit with our first piece so that the pattern continues around and around without stopping. Let's see if we can do this. I will start us out, and your job will be to add cars to the train. I have a *particular* train in my mind, and I want you to finish *my* train.

After a circular train is completed, the "take-away" and/or "fix-it" activities can be used, as in the Trains Level 1 modeling activity (see page 57). You may wish to use one of the patterns from the following activity pages as your model.

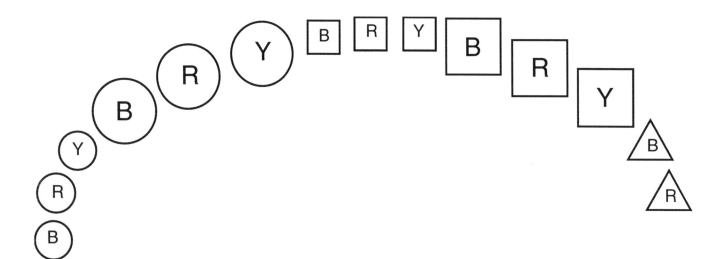

LEVEL 2–Activities

Teacher: For each activity, arrange the partial train as shown and give oral directions (shown in bold). Responses may be recorded on the lines.

Finish building the train so that it uses all 24 blocks.

1.

_____

_____

2.

_____

_____

3.

_____

LEVEL 2-Activities

Teacher: For each activity, arrange the partial train as shown and give oral directions (shown in bold). Responses may be recorded on the lines.

Finish building the train so that it uses all 24 blocks.

4.

_____

5.

_____

6.

_____

LEVEL 2-Activities

Teacher: For each activity, arrange the partial train as shown and give oral directions (shown in bold). Responses may be recorded on the lines.

Finish building the train so that it uses all 24 blocks.

7.

_____

_____

8.

_____

_____

9.

_____

_____

LEVEL 2-Activities

Teacher: Arrange the partial train as shown, and give oral directions (shown in bold).

10.   Finish building the circular train so that it uses all 24 blocks.

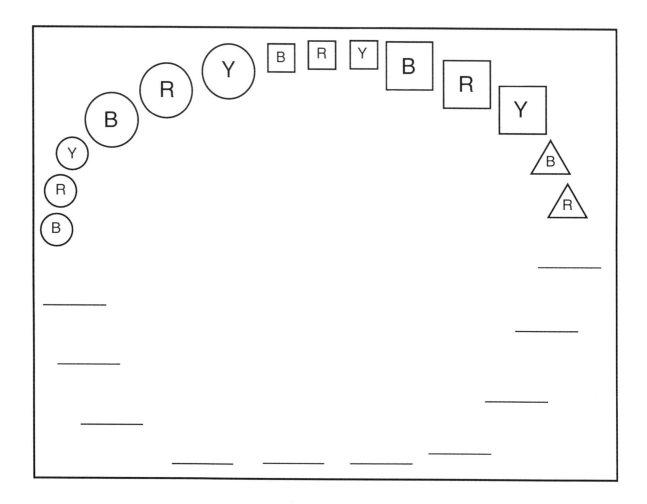

LEVEL 2-Activities

Teacher: Arrange the partial train as shown, and give oral directions (shown in bold).

11.   **Finish building the circular train so that it uses all 24 blocks.**

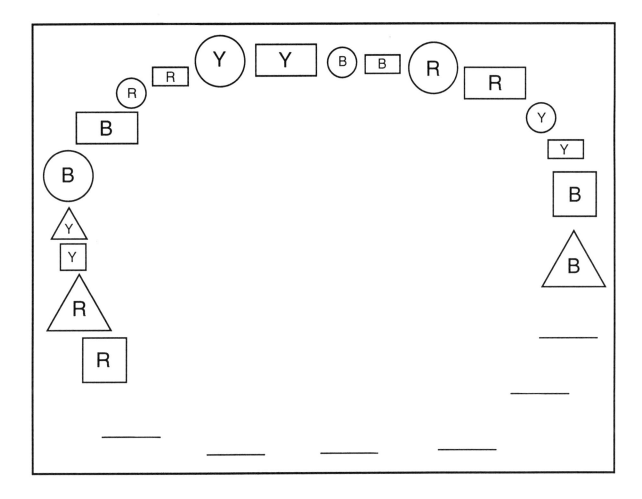

LEVEL 2-Activities

Teacher: Arrange the partial train as shown, and give oral directions (shown in bold).

12.   **Finish building the circular train so that it uses all 24 blocks.**

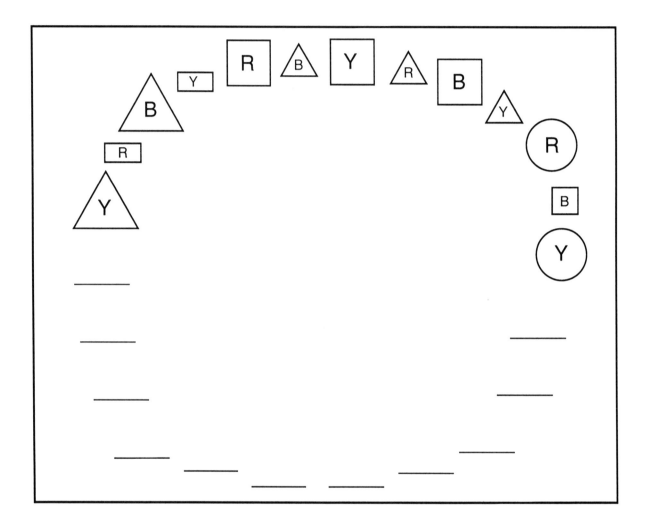

LEVEL 2-Activities

Teacher: Arrange both partial trains as shown, and give oral directions (shown in bold).

13. Finish building each 12-block circular train so that, together, they use all 24 blocks.

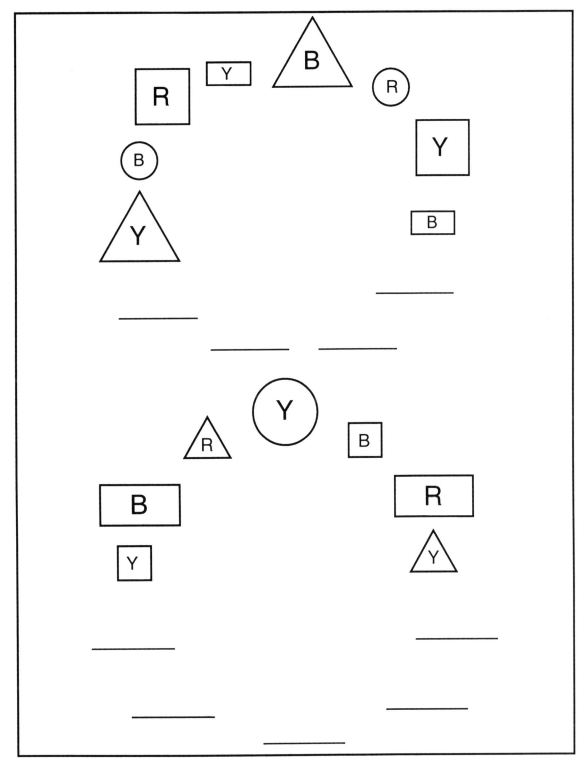

LEVEL 2-Activities

Teacher: Arrange both partial trains as shown, and give oral directions (shown in bold).

14. Finish building each 12-block circular train so that, together, they use all 24 blocks.

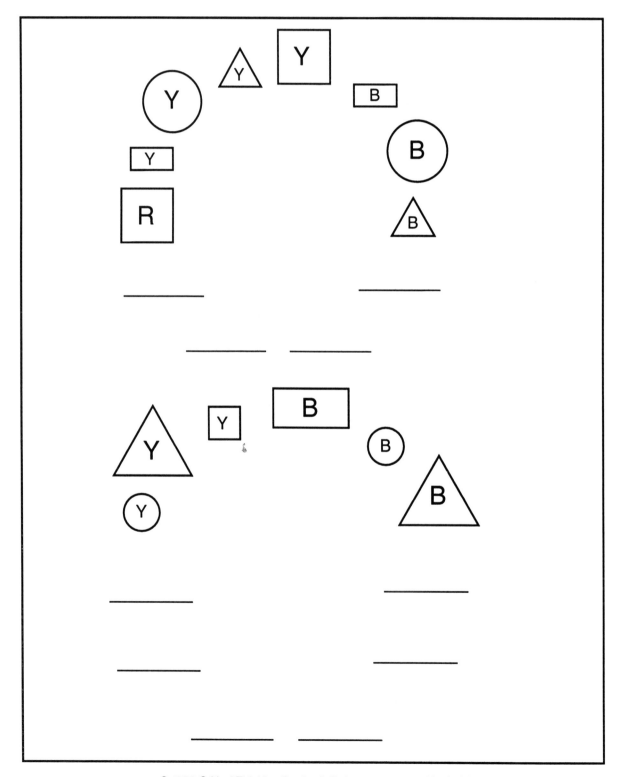

LEVEL 2-Assessment

Teacher: For each activity, arrange the partial train as shown, and give oral directions (shown in bold). Blanks may be used to record student responses.

Add three more cars to the train, keeping the pattern.

1.    _____ _____ _____

2.    _____ _____ _____

LEVEL 2-Assessment

Teacher: Arrange the partial train as shown, and give oral directions (shown in bold).
Blanks may be used to record student responses.

3.   Finish building the circular train so that it uses all 24 blocks.

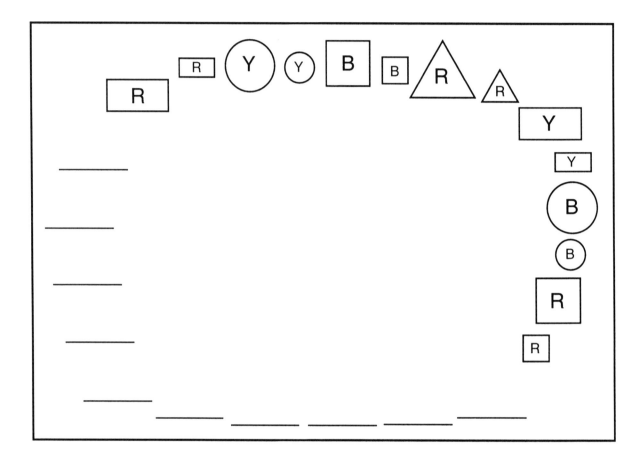

LEVEL 2-Assessment

Teacher: Arrange both partial trains as shown, and give oral directions (shown in bold). Blanks may be used to record student responses.

4.   Finish building each 12-block circular train so that, together, they use all 24 blocks.

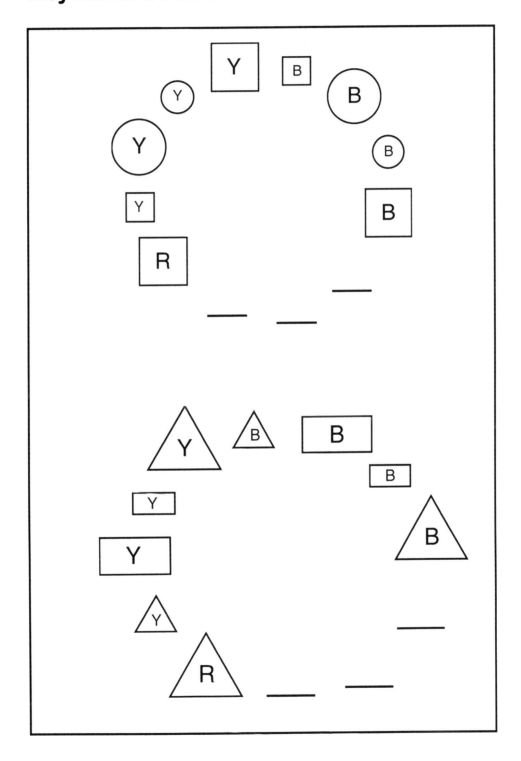

LEVEL 2-Assessment

Teacher: Arrange the partial train as shown, and give oral directions (shown in bold). Blanks may be used for student responses.

5.   Add the missing cars for the train, keeping the pattern.

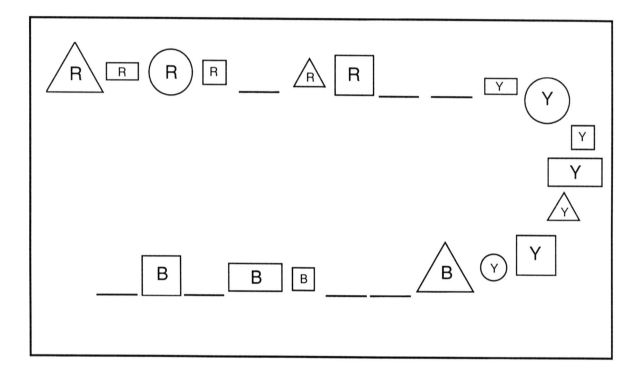

LEVEL 2-Assessment

Teacher: Arrange the partial train as shown, and give oral directions (shown in bold). Blanks may be used for student responses.

6.   Fix the train so it keeps its pattern.

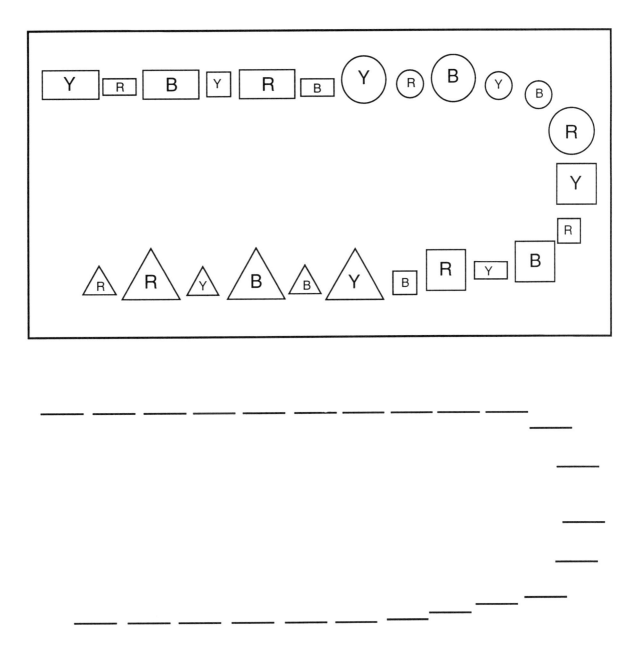

TRAINS LEVEL 3

Modeling Activity

PREPARATION

For this activity, you will need a thirty-block set: five shapes, three colors, two sizes.

Have the students seated in a circle with a large open space in the middle. In the center of the space, you will start a pattern "train" of blocks and place as many cars as required for the students to recognize the emerging pattern.

LESSON

The modeling activity given in Level 2 is also appropriate for this section. The only difference is the addition of one block, hexagon-shaped, for each color and size.

LEVEL 3-Activities

Teacher: For each activity, arrange the partial train as shown and give oral directions (shown in bold). Responses may be recorded on the lines.

Finish building the train so that it uses all 30 blocks and keeps the pattern.

1.

_____

_____

2.

_____

_____

3.

_____

_____

LEVEL 3–Activities

Teacher: For each activity, arrange the partial train as shown and give oral directions (shown in bold). Responses may be recorded on the lines.

Finish building the train so that it uses all 30 blocks and keeps the pattern.

4. B B Y Y R R B B Y Y R R B

5.

6. B Y R B Y R B Y R B

LEVEL 3-Activities

Teacher: For each activity, arrange the partial train as shown and give oral directions (shown in bold). Responses may be recorded on the lines.

Finish building the train so that it uses all 30 blocks and keeps the pattern.

7.

8.

9.

LEVEL-3 Activities

Teacher: For each activity, arrange the partial train as shown and give oral directions (shown in bold). Note: Blocks shown in activity 10 are all small.

Finish building the train so that it uses all 30 blocks and keeps the pattern.

10.

11.

12.

LEVEL 3-Activities

Teacher: For each activity, arrange the partial train as shown and give oral directions (shown in bold). Responses may be recorded on the lines.

Finish building the train so that it uses all 30 blocks and keeps the pattern.

13.

14.

15.

LEVEL 3-Activities

Teacher: For each activity, arrange the partial train as shown and give oral directions (shown in bold). Responses may be recorded on the lines.

16.   **Finish building the train so that it uses all 30 blocks and keeps the pattern.**

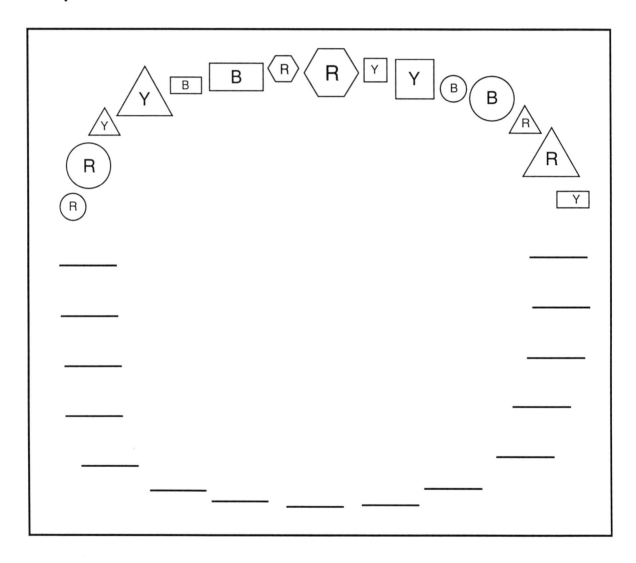

LEVEL 3-Activities

Teacher: For each activity, arrange the partial train as shown and give oral directions (shown in bold).

17.   Finish building the circular train so that it uses all 30 blocks.

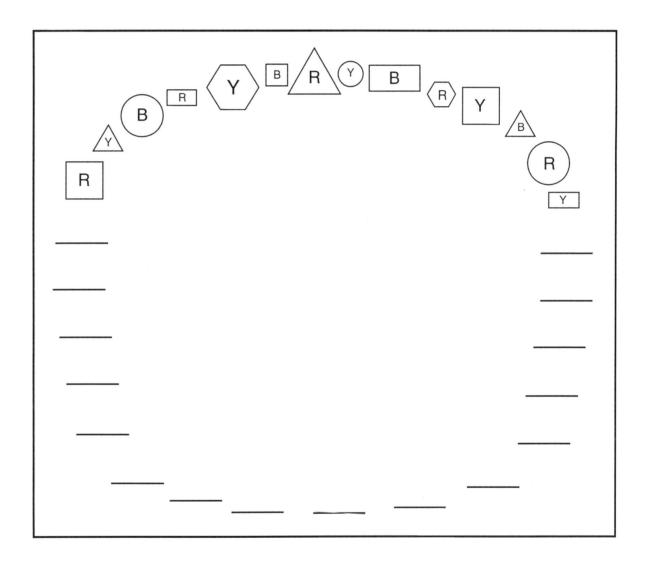

LEVEL 3-Activities

Teacher: For each activity, arrange the partial train as shown and give oral directions (shown in bold).

18.   **Finish building the circular train so that it uses all 30 blocks.**

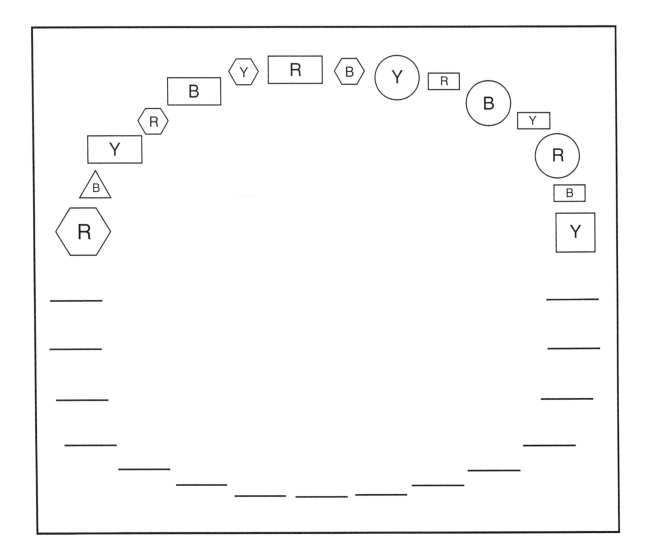

LEVEL 3-Activities

Teacher: For each activity, arrange the partial train as shown and give oral directions (shown in bold).

19.   Finish building the circular train so that it uses all 30 blocks.

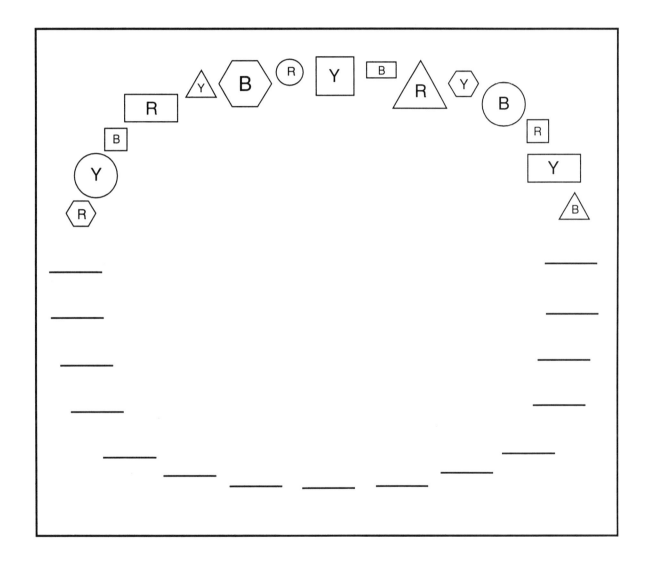

LEVEL 3-Activities

Teacher: For each activity, arrange the partial train as shown and give oral directions (shown in bold).

20.   Finish building the circular train so that it uses all 30 blocks.

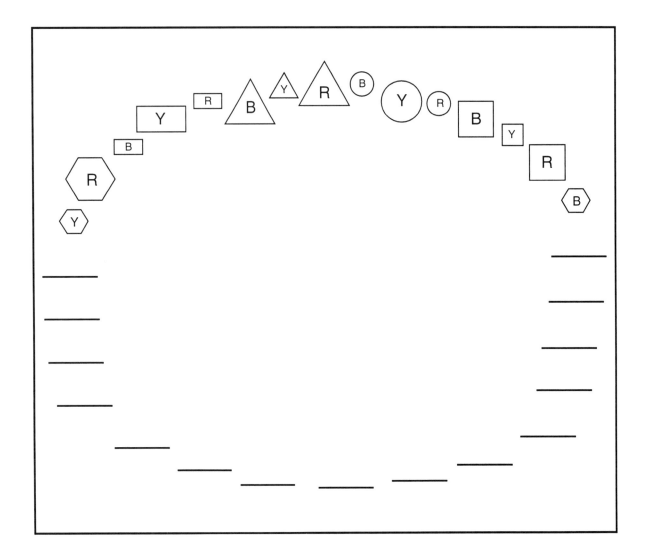

LEVEL 3–Assessment

Teacher: For each activity, arrange the partial train as shown, and give oral directions (shown in bold). Blanks may be used to record student responses.

Add three more cars to the train, keeping the pattern.

1.  ___ ___ ___

2.  ___ ___ ___

3. ___ ___ ___

LEVEL 3-Assessment

Teacher: Arrange the partial train as shown, and give oral directions (shown in bold). Responses may be recorded on the lines. Note that all blocks shown are small.

4.   **Finish building the train so that it uses all 30 blocks and keeps the pattern.**

_____

_____

LEVEL 3-Assessment

Teacher: Arrange the partial train as shown and give oral directions (shown in bold).

5.

Finish building the circular train so that it uses all 30 blocks and keeps the pattern.

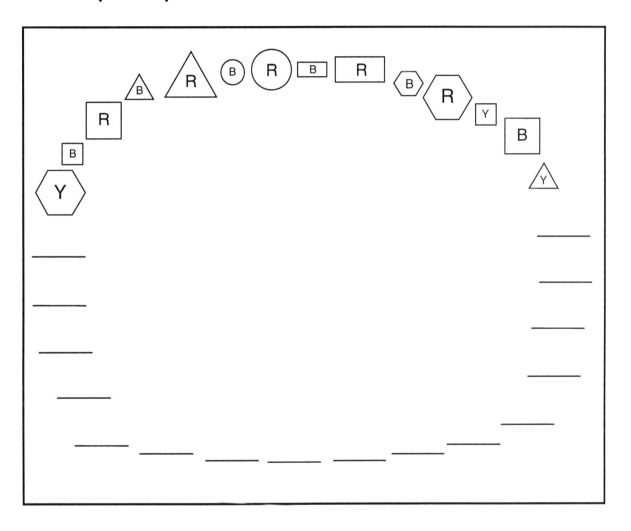

LEVEL 3-Assessment

Teacher: Arrange the partial train as shown, and give oral directions (shown in bold). Blanks may be used for student responses.

6. Add the missing cars for the train, keeping the pattern.

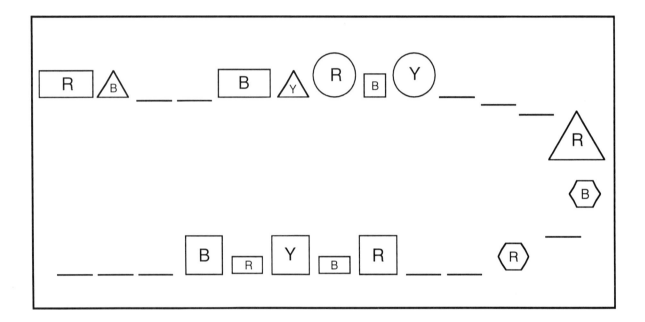

LEVEL 3-Assessment

Teacher: Arrange the partial train as shown, and give oral directions (shown in bold).
Blanks may be used for student responses.

7.   Fix the train so it keeps its pattern.

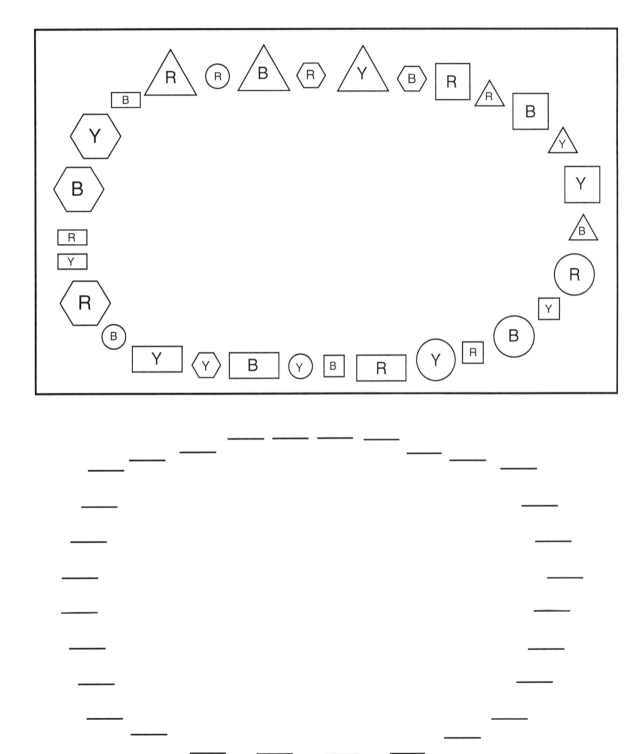

RINGS LEVEL 1

Modeling Activity

PREPARATION

You will need a set of twenty-four attribute blocks (four shapes, three colors, two sizes); chalk and chalkboard; several pieces of yarn (*not* red, blue, or yellow) each approximately 5 feet long; 9 same-size index cards—you will label each with one of the attributes listed below (cards should not be labelled with a marker that shows through the other side):

Attributes		
Color	**Shape**	**Size**
red	circle	large
blue	square	small
yellow	triangle	
	rectangle	

Spread the twenty-four blocks in the center of the floor space.

Have the students seated in a circle so that all can see the blocks in the center. You will show the cards and list attributes on the board.

The first part of the opening activity is very basic, though those with learning disabilities may find it a challenge.

LESSON

We are going to work with these special blocks, often called attribute blocks. There are twenty-four blocks in all. Who can give me the three different colors of these blocks?

Red, blue, yellow.

Good. I will list these colors here on the board.

List colors on the board, and write each on a card.

I have also made a card for each color. Now, who can give me the names of the four shapes?

Circle, square, triangle, rectangle.

In working with young children, refer to the shapes of the blocks as squares, circles, triangles, and rectangles (the shapes of the *surfaces*). Using the terms associated with three dimensions (cylinders, rectangular solids, triangular prisms, etc.) can lead to confusion.

Good. I will list these shapes on the board, too, and I also have a card for each shape.

List shapes on the board, and write each on a card.

Finally, what are the two sizes of the blocks?

Large, small.

OK, I will list these two sizes on the board and also on two cards.

List the sizes large and small on the board, and write each on a card.

The introduction of the nine attributes and their precise use in naming each block is fundamental for the activities that follow. If word recognition is difficult, colors and shape designs can be substituted for the printed words. It is important for students to understand that there is one word for each card, not a combination of attributes. The listing of the attributes on the board provides a reference for the students.

Now we have three colors, four shapes, and two sizes. Each block has a unique name that uses one of each of these attributes.

Choose any block and ask its name.

What is the exact name of this block?

Prompt as necessary to get the 3-attribute name for the block; when the correct name has been found, pick another block.

What about this block? I will go around the circle and let each of you give me the name of the block I choose for your turn.

Ask similar questions until each student has given an answer. Then follow the dialogue below, making a circle with yarn, next to the blocks, and placing attribute cards and blocks as described.

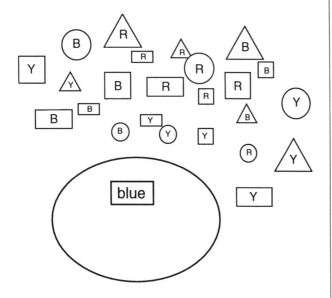

Now, in this empty space next to the blocks, I will make a ring with yarn. I will choose one of the nine attribute cards and place that card face up within the ring. Since I've chosen "blue," all the *blue* blocks belong within the ring.

[Noah], will you come up and put all the blue blocks in their correct place?

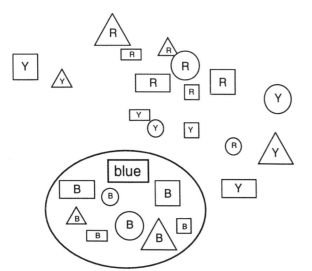

Good. How many blocks are inside the ring?

Eight.

How many blocks are outside the ring?

Sixteen.

What can we call the blocks outside the ring?

They are "not blue."

OK, I am going to change the card. I will put all the blue blocks back with the rest of the blocks. This time, I will put a different attribute card (triangle) in the ring. Who can come up and put the correct blocks in the ring?

Have a student put the correct blocks inside the ring:

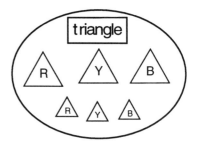

Now begins an exciting part of the ring challenges: identifying the attribute of a ring when the card is placed *face down* in the ring.

This activity will grow in difficulty so that when students reach Book B, it will be a very complex challenge. For now, mastering the simple version is all that is important.

Now, I am going to give you a challenge. I will put all the blocks here in this space, and we will start with no blocks in the ring. I will choose one of the nine attribute cards, as I have been doing, but this time I will not show you the word on the card. Instead, I will put the card face down in the ring like this.

Place the "red" card face down in the ring.

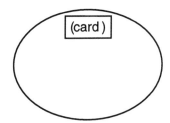

Your challenge is to tell me the name of this card, not by guessing, but by using the blocks. I will choose one block at a time and I will place that block in the ring if it belongs there, or outside the ring if it does not belong in the ring. After I have checked several blocks, you can tell me the name of the card.

I will start with the large blue circle. This block does not belong in the ring, so I will place it outside the ring.

Place blocks, step by step, as shown in the diagram. As leader, you must always be sure to place the block in the correct location. The activity will not work successfully if a block is in the wrong place!

Next, I will check the large red circle. This block goes in the ring. What about the large red triangle? It goes in. And the large red rectangle? It belongs inside, too. And the small red square…that one also goes in the circle!

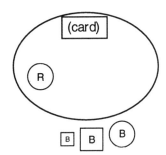

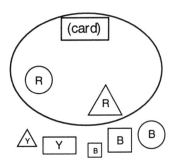

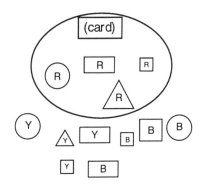

What do you think the card says?

Red!

Good, you are correct. The card has to say red in order to belong in the ring. Let's check and see if we are correct

Turn over the card.

Yes. We are right.

The number of blocks needed to establish the identity of the card will vary among student groups. Older children will usually quickly know the answer, whereas younger students or those with learning disabilities will need more blocks before they can see the answer. The number of blocks used is not important; it is the critical thinking involved in the activity that is important.

Let's try this again using a different card.

Choose another attribute card and lead the students as before.

As students master the activity, let them choose each successive block to be tested, as below. The question, What is the best block to check? begins to emerge.

Good. You are really doing very well. Let me change one thing this time. We will clear the space and, again, I will choose a card and place it face down in the ring. But this time, *you* will tell me which block to check. We will go around the circle so that on your turn, you may choose a block to check. After I place the block in the correct space, you may tell me the name of the card if you think you know what it is. If

you are not sure, we will go to the next student in our circle.

Continue so that all students have sufficient opportunity to choose blocks and guess the card names.

After only a few blocks have been checked, the deeper question, "What are all the possible answers at this point?" can become very challenging. As students choose the block to be checked, you can, if appropriate, ask questions like the following:

Why did you choose that block?

What are you trying to find out?

What do you think that card might say?

What information will help you find the name of that card?

Before you choose a block to be checked, what are all the possible answers at this point?

Many children will choose blocks on a random basis at the beginning of this type of activity, and many will continue to do so. It will only begin to evolve that the choice of block takes on an important role in solving the challenge efficiently (fewest number of blocks needed). This does not seem to be a vital skill with young children and should not take on a significance out of proportion to their age group. Teachers can use all of these activities as an effective maturity assessment instrument.

As demonstrated, this beginning activity can go from simple to complex, all by using only one ring.

LEVEL 1-Activities

Teacher: For each activity, place the appropriate card in a ring of yarn and give oral directions (shown in bold). Provide the set of 24 blocks.

1. Look at the attribute card in the ring. Correctly place three blocks inside this ring.

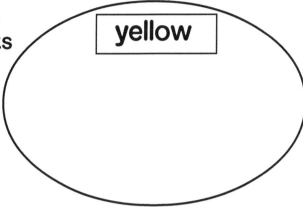

2. Look at the attribute card in the ring. Correctly place four blocks inside this ring.

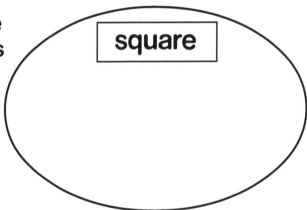

3. Look at the attribute card in the ring. Correctly place five blocks inside this ring.

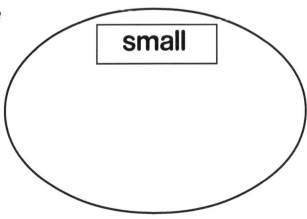

LEVEL 1-Activities

Teacher: For each activity, place the appropriate card in a ring of yarn and give oral directions (shown in bold). Provide the set of 24 blocks.

4. Look at the attribute card in the ring. Correctly place six blocks inside the ring.

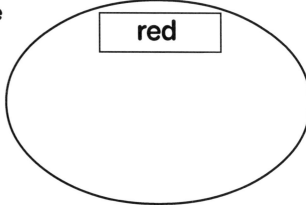

5. Look at the attribute card in the ring. Correctly place inside the ring all blocks that belong.

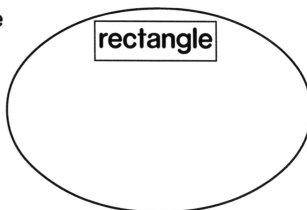

6. Look at the attribute card in the ring. Correctly place inside the ring all blocks that belong.

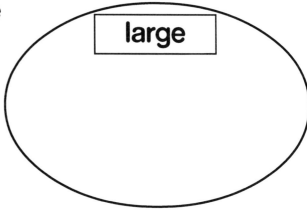

LEVEL 1-Activities

Teacher: For each activity, place the appropriate card in a ring of yarn and give oral directions (shown in bold). Provide the set of 24 blocks.

7. Look at the attribute card in the ring. Correctly place three blocks *outside* the ring.

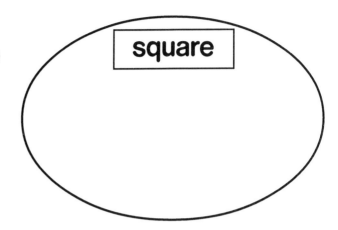

8. Look at the attribute card in the ring. Correctly place four blocks *outside* the ring.

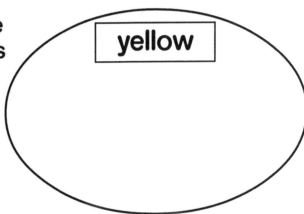

9. Look at the attribute card in the ring. Correctly place five blocks *outside* the ring.

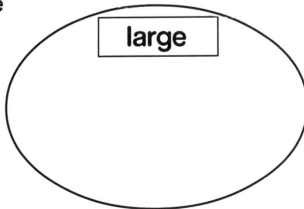

LEVEL 1-Activities

Teacher: For each activity, place the appropriate card in a ring of yarn and give oral directions (shown in bold). Provide the set of 24 blocks.

10. Look at the attribute card in the ring. Correctly place outside the ring all the blocks that do not belong.

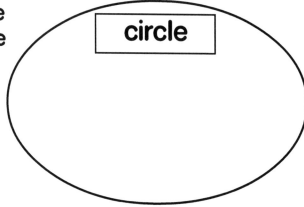

11. Look at the attribute card in the ring. Correctly place three blocks inside the ring and three of the 24 blocks outside the ring.

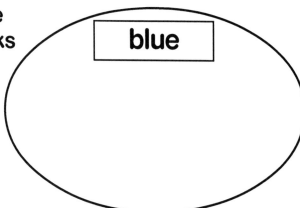

12. Look at the attribute card in the ring. Correctly place four blocks inside the ring and four blocks outside the ring.

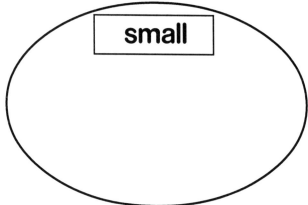

LEVEL 1-Activities

Teacher: For each activity, place the appropriate card in a ring of yarn and give oral directions (shown in bold). Provide the set of 24 blocks.

13. Look at the attribute card in the ring. Correctly place five blocks inside the ring and five blocks outside the ring.

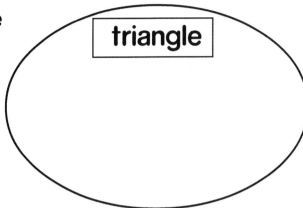

14. Look at the attribute card in the ring. Correctly place all blocks, either inside or outside the ring, according to the card.

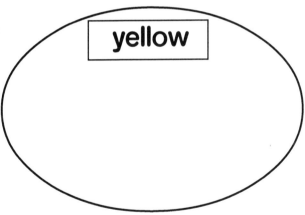

LEVEL 1-Activities

Teacher: For each activity, arrange blocks in a ring of yarn as shown and give oral directions (shown in bold).

15 a. What is the name of the attribute card for this ring?

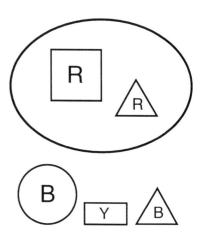

b. What is the name of the attribute card for this ring?

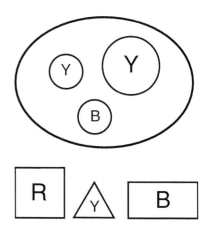

c. What is the name of the attribute card for this ring?

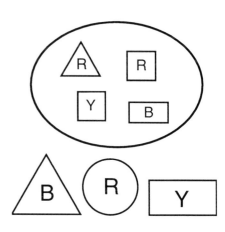

LEVEL 1-Activities

Teacher: For each activity, arrange blocks in a ring of yarn as shown and give oral directions (shown in bold).

15 d. What is the name of the attribute card for this ring?

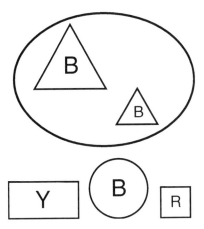

e. What is the name of the attribute card for this ring?

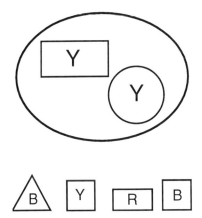

f. What is the name of the attribute card for this ring?

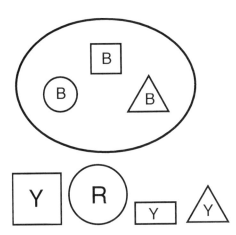

LEVEL 1-Activities

Teacher: For each activity, arrange blocks in a ring of yarn as shown and give oral directions (shown in bold).

16 a. What are all the possible names for the attribute card for this ring?

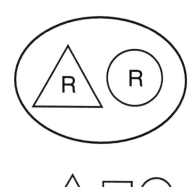

b. What are all the possible names for the attribute card for this ring?

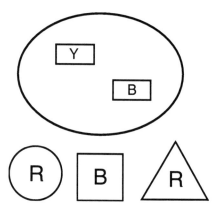

c. What are all the possible names for the attribute card for this ring?

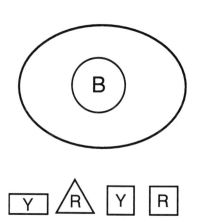

LEVEL 1-Activities

Teacher: For each activity, arrange blocks in a ring of yarn as shown and give oral directions (shown in bold). Note: there is more than one correct answer.

17 a. What block would you choose next so you would know the name for the attribute card?

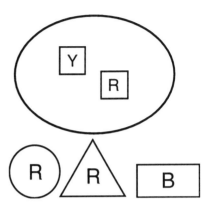

b. What block would you choose next so you would know the name for the attribute card?

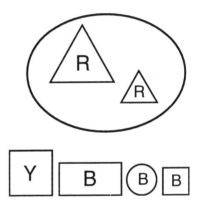

c. What block would you choose next so you would know the name for the attribute card?

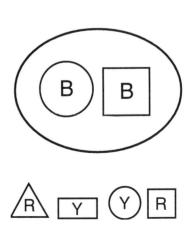

LEVEL 1-Assessments

Teacher: For each activity, place the appropriate card in a ring of yarn and give oral directions (shown in bold). Provide the set of 24 blocks.

1. Look at the attribute card in the ring. Correctly place three blocks inside the ring.

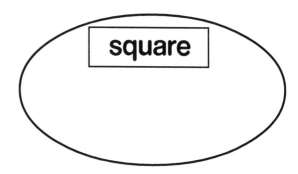

2. Look at the attribute card in the ring. Correctly place three blocks outside the ring.

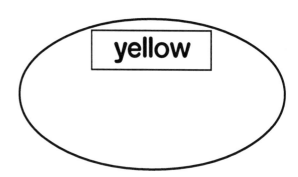

3. Look at the attribute card in the ring. Correctly place three blocks inside the ring and three blocks outside the ring.

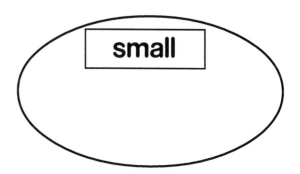

LEVEL 1-Assessments

Teacher: For each activity, arrange blocks in a ring of yarn as shown and give oral directions (shown in bold).

4. **What is the name of the attribute card for labelling this ring?**

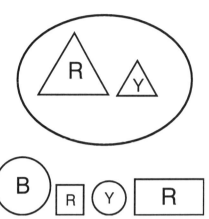

5. **What are all possible names for the attribute card to label this ring?**

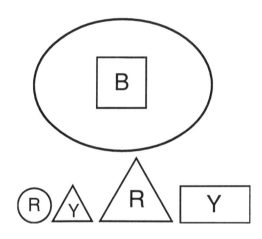

6. **What is one possible block you could choose next to learn the name of the attribute card for this ring?**

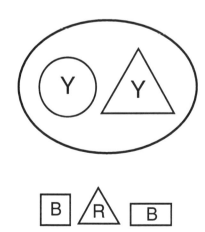

RINGS LEVEL 2

Modeling Activity

PREPARATION

You will need a set of set of thirty attribute blocks (five shapes, three colors, two sizes); chalk and chalkboard; several pieces of yarn (*not* red, blue, or yellow) each approximately 5 feet long; 9 same-size index cards—you will label each with one of the attributes (cards should not be labelled with a marker that shows through the other side).

Attributes

Color	Shape	Size
red	circle	large
blue	square	small
yellow	triangle	
	rectangle	
	hexagon	

This level of Rings uses activities similar to those in the previous level, but now you will include six hexagons (two sizes of each of the three colors).

LESSON

Review and summarize the previous level's activities.

We have already worked with a set of 24 blocks when we used the yarn rings and the cards. We decided which blocks to place in the labelled rings. We also labelled the rings that had blocks inside and out.

You may wish to ask students to remember more and tell what they remember about the ring activities before going on to 30-block activities.

Today, we are going to do some more activities like that, but with one change: instead of just twenty-four blocks, we will use *thirty*. This set includes the hexagon.

If the students have not yet used the hexagon-shaped block, show one or more of the 6 hexagons (three colors, two sizes).

The hexagon has six sides. Like the other shapes, the hexagons come in all three colors: red, yellow, and blue. Each color of hexagon comes in a large or small size.

The activities that follow should be completed the same way as those of Level 1.

LEVEL 2-Activities

Teacher: For each activity, place the appropriate card in a ring of yarn and give oral directions (shown in bold). Provide the set of 30 blocks.

1. Look at the attribute card in the ring. Correctly place three blocks in this ring.

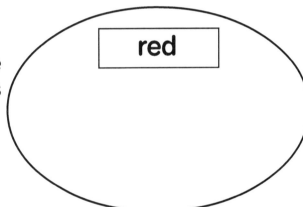

2. Look at the attribute card in the ring. Correctly place four blocks in this ring.

3. Look at the attribute card in the ring. Correctly place five blocks in this ring.

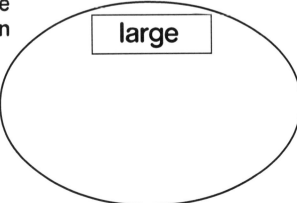

LEVEL 2-Activities

Teacher: For each activity, place the appropriate card in a ring of yarn and give oral directions (shown in bold). Provide the set of 30 blocks.

4. Look at the attribute card in the ring. Correctly place six blocks in this ring.

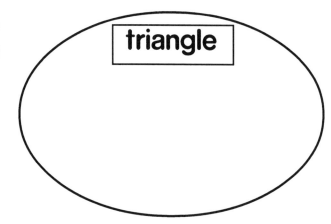

5. Look at the attribute card in the ring. Correctly place in this ring all the blocks that belong.

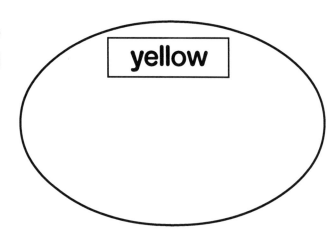

6. Look at the attribute card in the ring. Correctly place in this ring all the blocks that belong.

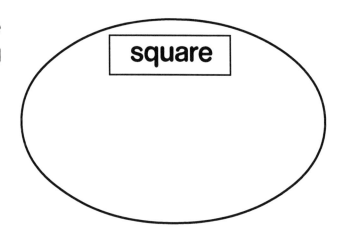

LEVEL 2-Activities

Teacher: For each activity, place the appropriate card in a ring of yarn and give oral directions (shown in bold). Provide the set of 30 blocks.

7. Look at the attribute card in the ring. Correctly place three blocks outside the ring.

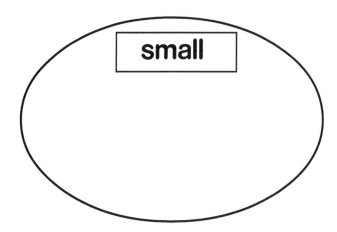

8. Look at the attribute card in the ring. Correctly place four blocks outside the ring.

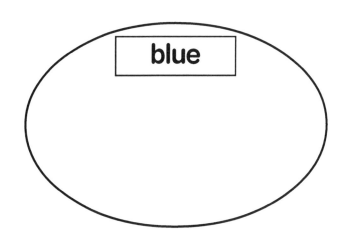

9. Look at the attribute card in the ring. Correctly place five blocks outside the ring.

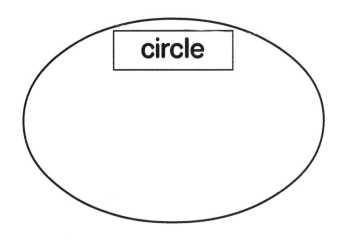

LEVEL 2-Activities

Teacher: For each activity, place the appropriate card in a ring of yarn and give oral directions (shown in bold). Provide the set of 30 blocks.

10. Look at the attribute card in the ring. Correctly place outside the ring all the blocks that do not belong.

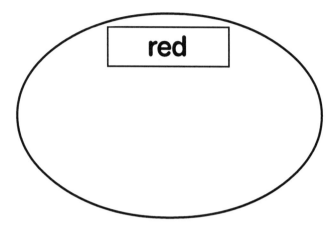

11. Look at the attribute card in the ring. Correctly place three blocks inside the ring and three blocks outside the ring.

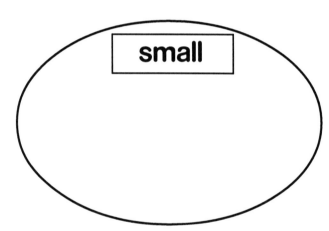

12. Look at the attribute card in the ring. Correctly place four blocks inside the ring and four blocks outside the ring.

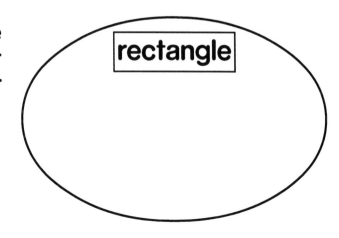

LEVEL 2-Activities

Teacher: For each activity, place the appropriate card in a ring of yarn and give oral directions (shown in bold). Provide the set of 30 blocks.

13. Look at the attribute card in the ring. Correctly place five blocks inside the ring and five blocks outside the ring.

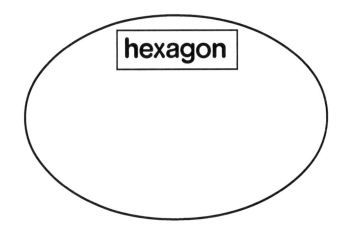

14. Look at the attribute card in the ring. Correctly place each of the 30 blocks either inside the ring or outside the ring.

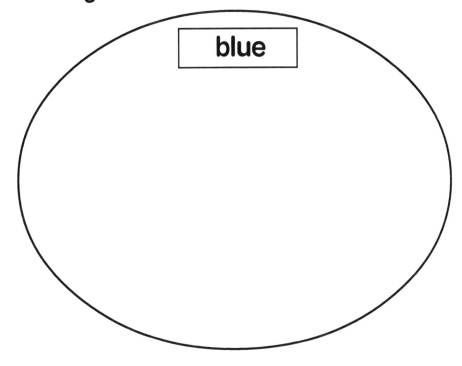

LEVEL 2-Activities

Teacher: For each activity, place the appropriate card in a ring of yarn and give oral directions (shown in bold). Provide the set of 30 blocks.

15 a. What is the name of the attribute card for this ring?

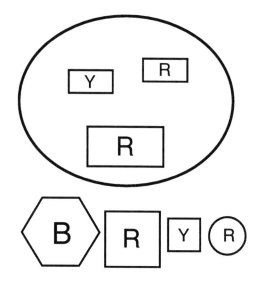

b. What is the name of the attribute card for this ring?

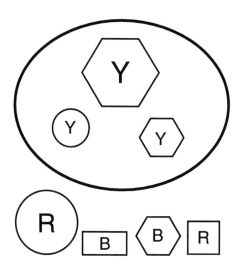

c. What is the name of the attribute card for this ring?

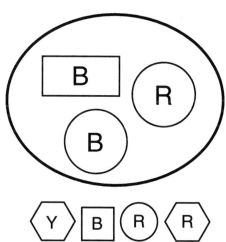

LEVEL 2-Activities

Teacher: For each activity, arrange blocks in a ring of yarn as shown and give oral directions (shown in bold).

15 d. What is the name of the attribute card for this ring?

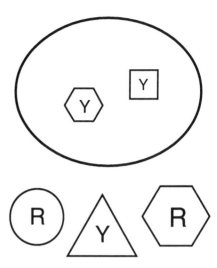

e. What is the name of the attribute card for this ring?

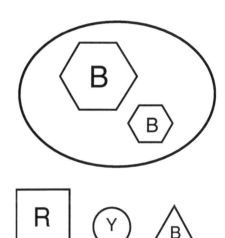

f. What is the name of the attribute card for this ring?

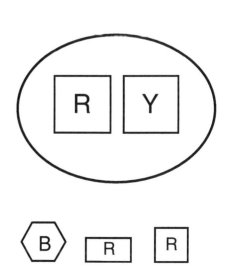

LEVEL 2-Activities

Teacher: For each activity, arrange blocks in a ring of yarn as shown and give oral directions (shown in bold).

16 a. What are all the possible names for the attribute card for this ring?

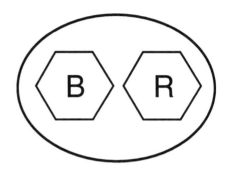

b. What are all the possible names for the attribute card for this ring?

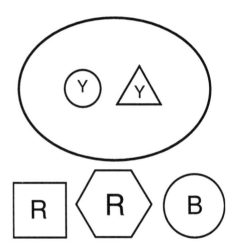

c. What are all the possible names for the attribute card for this ring?

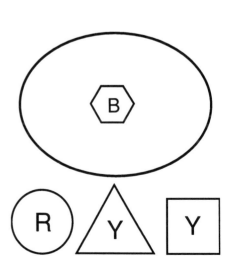

LEVEL 2-Activities

Teacher: For each activity, arrange blocks in a ring of yarn as shown and give oral directions (shown in bold). Note: there is more than one correct answer.

17 a. **What block would you choose next so you would know the name for the attribute card?**

b. **What block would you choose next so you would know the name for the attribute card?**

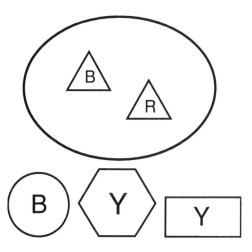

c. **What block would you choose next so you would know the name for the attribute card?**

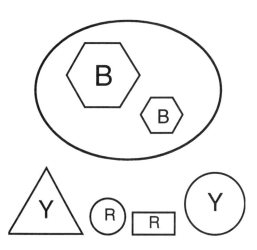

LEVEL 2-Assessments

Teacher: For each activity, place the appropriate card in a ring of yarn and give oral directions (shown in bold). Provide the set of 30 blocks.

1. **Look at the attribute card in the ring. Correctly place three blocks inside the ring.**

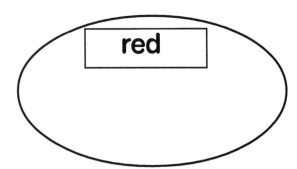

2. **Look at the attribute card in the ring. Correctly place three blocks outside the ring.**

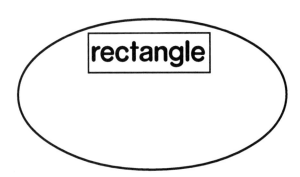

3. **Look at the attribute card in the ring. Correctly place three blocks inside the ring and three blocks outside the ring.**

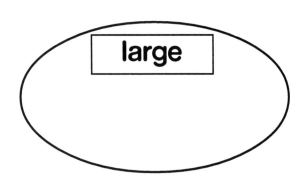

LEVEL 2-Assessments

Teacher: For each activity, arrange blocks in a ring of yarn as shown and give oral directions (shown in bold).

4. **What is the name of the attribute card for this ring?**

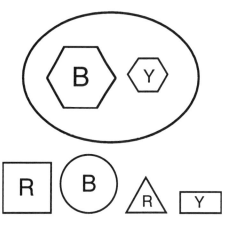

5. **What are all possible names for the attribute cards to label this ring?**

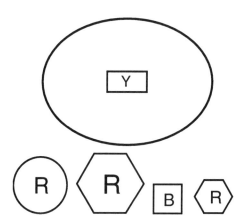

6. **What is one possible block you could choose next so that you would know the name of the attribute card for this ring?**

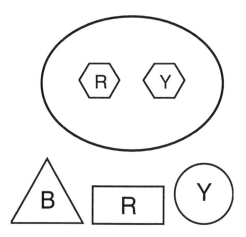

MYSTERY BLOCKS LEVEL 1
Modeling Activity

PREPARATION

You will need a set of twenty-four attribute blocks: four shapes, three colors, two sizes. Before the session, write the attributes of the twenty-four blocks on the board where students can see the list:

Attributes		
Color	**Shape**	**Size**
red	circle	large
blue	square	small
yellow	triangle	
	rectangle	

In this activity, you will choose one block from the set without telling what block it is. You will write the name of the mystery block (i.e., large red circle) on paper for an element of drama and to prevent students from thinking that you are changing the name of the mystery block during the course of the activity. Students will ask yes-or-no questions to determine the identity of the chosen block; they will proceed to sort blocks according to the answers until they arrive at the one block you had chosen.

Before the session, or as students arrive, spread the 24 blocks in the center floor space. Have the students seated in a circle so that everyone can see the blocks.

LESSON

I want to first place all twenty-four of our attribute blocks here in this open space on the floor. Can you all see all the blocks? Good. Now I am going to write the name of one of the blocks here on my paper; I will be the only one who knows the name of the mystery block. Remember, each block has three parts to its name: its size, its shape, and its color. I have listed these attributes here on the board as a reminder for all of us.

Sorting the blocks is very important in the beginning, especially if students are not familiar with the blocks. It is also crucial for those who still need concrete activities before going on to more abstract levels of problem solving. Later, students may be able to sort the blocks mentally or use paper/pencil.

Now, you are going to find the name of my mystery block by asking me questions that I can answer with a "yes" or a "no." Your question can ask me about any one of the attributes listed on the board. When I give you the answer to your question, I want you to go to the blocks and sort the blocks into two piles: the blocks that *are* possibly the mystery block and those that *cannot* be the mystery block.

Make sure students understand the rules of the activity, giving them an example if necessary. (At first, it is productive to ask about one attribute only: "Is the block a *large* one?"— NOT "Is it a *large yellow* block ?")

Let's begin. You will catch on very quickly. I have written the name of the mystery block here on my paper. Who will ask the first question? Okay, [Amanda.]

The following hypothetical scenario will give you an idea of how to proceed, even though actual questions and sorting arrangements will differ.

Is it red?

No, the mystery block is not red. Will you sort the blocks into two piles? Over here will be the blocks that *can* be the mystery block and here will be the blocks that *cannot* be the mystery block.

Yes   No

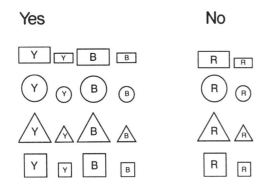

Good, [Amanda]. Do you all agree with the sorting that [Amanda] has done?

The students should see that the second sorting is a continuation of the first sorting and we will continue to eliminate blocks from the Possible Mystery Block pile until we are left with our answer. This is the procedure we will follow as we progress through the entire sequence of mystery block activities, from simple to abstract.

Now, who has the next question about the mystery block?

Is it a triangle?

No, the mystery block is not a triangle. [Giovanni], will you now make the changes with the blocks to show which ones can still be the mystery block and which ones cannot be the mystery block?

Yes   No

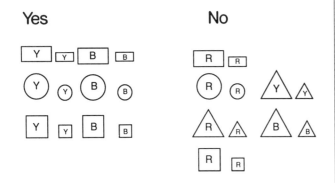

Good work. Do you all agree that the mystery block must be in this collection of blocks?

[Heather], do you have a yes/no question for me?

Is it yellow?

Yes, the mystery block is yellow. Can you make the needed changes with the blocks to show this?

Yes   No

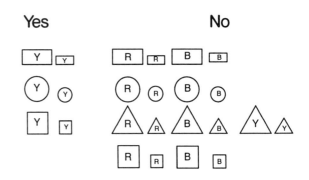

Good. The mystery block must be in this collection of blocks. I wonder which one it is.

Is it large?

No, the mystery block is not a large block. What can you do with the blocks now? Show me the blocks that can still be the mystery block.

Yes   No

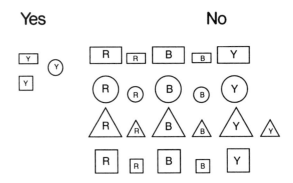

Good work [Jacqueline]. So now we are down to these three blocks. Who wants to ask the next question?

Is it a circle?

Yes. It is the small yellow circle. Good. We have found the mystery block. Are there any questions?

The yes/no questioning is a good experience for the higher order processing involved in continually cutting a set into halves to find the hidden element.

You can continue with the same activity, choosing a different mystery block, if you feel the students need more experiences of this kind. When the students are ready to proceed, continue with the following extension of the original activity.

In the beginning, present clues one at a time. Sort the blocks after each clue is given (see arrangements for each step).

Now I am going to give you a set of answers to your yes/no question. I will call these the "clues" to my mystery block. Each clue is really an answer to one of your possible questions. I want us to sort the blocks after each clue is given to show the possible mystery blocks.

Clue number one: The mystery block is not a square.

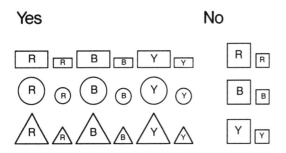

Clue number two: The mystery block is blue.

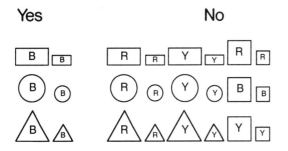

Clue number three: The mystery block is not a rectangle.

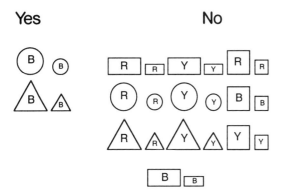

Clue number four: The mystery block is a circle.

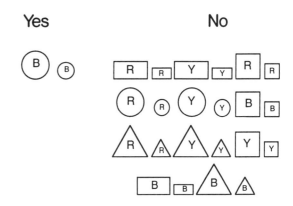

Clue number five: The mystery block is not small.

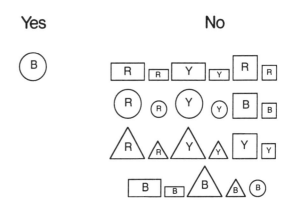

The mystery block is the large blue circle.

The order in which the clues are presented is not crucial. In fact, as we progress deeper into these challenges, it will become efficient to change the order, as some clues give more obvious information.

For more advanced students, this activity can be used as a cooperative learning experience. The ultimate group challenge is to separate the clues so that each student has one or two. Then, without showing their clues to each other, students must share their information to find the mystery block.

Now that you know how to work with clues, I want you to work in small groups. I will give you all the clues for a mystery block. I want you to work together to find the solution. You have the real blocks to work with if you need them. Are there any questions?

LEVEL 1-ACTIVITIES

Teacher: Cut clues in strips and divide among students. Give oral directions (shown in bold).

Sort the 24 blocks according to the clues until you find the mystery block.

1.   It is not yellow.

It is small.

It is not a circle.

It has four sides.

It is not a square.

It is red.

It is the

_____

2.   It is not a square.

It is not blue.

It is yellow.

It is not small.

It is not a circle.

It has three sides.

It is the

_____

3.   It is not a circle.

It has equal-length sides.

It is small.

It is not yellow.

It is blue.

It does not have four sides.

It is the

_____

4.   It is not three-sided.

It is large.

It has four sides.

It is not red.

It is not small.

It is yellow.

It is not a square.

It is the

_____

LEVEL 1-ACTIVITIES

Teacher: Cut clues in strips and divide among students. Give oral directions (shown in bold).

Sort the 24 blocks according to the clues until you find the mystery block.

5. It has four sides.

It is not blue.

It is not large.

It is not a circle.

It is small.

It is not a rectangle.

It is red.

It is the

_____

6. It is not a circle.

It has equal-length sides.

It is not small.

It is not yellow.

It is large.

It is blue.

It has an odd number of sides.

It is the

_____

7. It is not red.

It has equal-length sides.

It is not a circle.

It is not red.

It has an even number of sides.

It is large.

It is yellow.

It is the

_____

8. It is not small.

It has four corners.

It is not a circle.

It is not blue.

It does not have equal-length sides.

It is not yellow.

It is the

_____

LEVEL 1-ASSESSMENTS

Teacher: Cut clues in strips and divide among students. Give oral directions (shown in bold).

Sort the 24 blocks according to the clues until you find the mystery block. You may share information.

1.   It is not red.

It has four sides.

It is not large.

It is not a triangle.

It is small.

It is not a square.

It is not a circle.

It is blue.

It is the

_____

2.   It is not yellow.

It has equal-length sides.

It is not a circle.

It is red.

It is not large.

It has fewer than four corners.

It is the

_____

MYSTERY BLOCKS LEVEL 2
Modeling Activity

PREPARATION

You will need a set of thirty attribute blocks: five shapes, three colors, and two sizes. Before the session, write the attributes of the thirty blocks on the board where students can see the list:

Attributes		
Color	**Shape**	**Size**
red	circle	large
blue	square	small
yellow	triangle	
	rectangle	
	hexagon	

As you did in Level 1, you will choose one block from the set without telling what block it is. You will write the name of the mystery block (i.e., large red circle) on paper and students will ask yes-or-no questions to determine the identity of the chosen block; they will sort blocks until they arrive at the mystery block.

Before the session, or as students arrive, spread the 30 blocks in the center floor space.

Have students arranged in a circle so that everyone can see the blocks.

LESSON

Review and summarize the previous level's activities. (Then proceed with the Level 2 activities the same as you did Level 1.)

We have already worked with a set of 24 blocks when you asked yes-or-no questions to guess the mystery block.

(You may wish to ask students to remember more and tell what they remember about the Level 1 activities before going on to 30-block activities.)

Today, we are going to do some more activities like that, but with one change: instead of just twenty-four blocks, we will use *thirty*. This set includes the hexagon.

If the students have not yet used the hexagon-shaped block, show one or more of the 6 hexagons (three colors, two sizes).

The hexagon has six sides. Like the other shapes, the hexagons come in all three colors: red, yellow, and blue. Each color of hexagon comes in a large or small size.

The activities that follow should be completed the same way as those of Level 1.

LEVEL 2-ACTIVITIES

Teacher: Cut clues in strips and divide among students. Give oral directions (shown in bold).

Sort the 30 blocks according to the clues until you find the mystery block.

1. It is not yellow.

It has equal-length sides.

It is not small.

It is blue.

It does not have four sides.

It has fewer than five corners.

It is a

_____

2. It is not a circle.

It has equal-length sides.

It is not yellow.

It is not large.

It has more than three sides.

It is not red.

It has six corners.

It is a

_____

3. It is not red.

It has more than three sides.

It is small.

It has four corners

It is not blue.

It does not have equal-length sides.

It is a

_____

4. It is not small.

It has equal-length sides.

It is not yellow.

It has more than three corners.

It is not a circle.

It is blue.

It is not a square.

It is a

_____

LEVEL 2-ACTIVITIES

Teacher: Cut clues in strips and divide among students. Give oral directions (shown in bold).

Sort the 30 blocks according to the clues until you find the mystery block.

5. It has four sides.

It is not blue.

It is large.

It has equal-length sides.

It has four corners.

It is not yellow.

It is a

_____

6. It is not a triangle.

It is not red.

It is large.

It is not a square.

It is yellow.

It does not have six sides.

It is not a rectangle.

It is a

_____

7. It is not a circle.

It is small.

It does not have three sides.

It is not red.

It has equal-length sides.

It is yellow.

It has more than four corners.

It is a

_____

8. It is not blue.

It has equal-length sides.

It is not a circle.

It is not yellow.

It has an odd number of corners.

It is red.

It is not large.

It is a

_____

LEVEL 2-ASSESSMENTS

Teacher: Cut clues in strips and divide among students. Give oral directions (shown in bold).

Sort the 30 blocks according to the clues until you find the mystery block.

1. It does not have four sides.

It is not red.

It is not large.

It is blue.

It is not a triangle.

It has no corners.

It is a

_____

2. It is not a circle.

It has more than three sides.

It has equal-length sides.

It is not red.

It is large.

It has more than four corners.

It is not blue.

It is a

_____

ANSWERS

MATRICES

Matrices
Level 1—Activities

1a. Number: <u>4</u>

Names: <u>Small yellow triangle, large red circle, large blue square, small yellow rect-angle</u>

1b. Number: <u>5</u>

Names: <u>Large yellow triangle, small red tri-angle, large red square, large blue circle, small blue square</u>

1c. Number: <u>5</u>

Names: <u>Small red circle, small yellow square, large yellow triangle, small blue rect-angle, large blue circle</u>

1d. Number: <u>6</u>

Names: <u>Small blue rectangle, large red rect-angle, small yellow rectangle, small red circle, small yellow circle, large blue triangle</u>

2a.

2b.

2c.

2d.

Matrices
Level 1—Assessments

1a. Number: <u>3</u>

Names: <u>Small yellow triangle, large blue circle, large red square</u>

1b. Number: <u>5</u>

Names: <u>Large blue square, small yellow square, large yellow triangle, large blue tri-angle, small blue rectangle</u>

2a.

2b.

Matrices
Level 2—Activities

1a. Number: <u>5</u>

Names: <u>Small yellow square, small red triangle, large yellow square, small blue rectangle, large red triangle</u>

1b. Number: <u>6</u>

Names: <u>Small red triangle, large red triangle, small yellow circle, small yellow rectangle, large yellow square, small yellow square</u>

1c. Number: <u>6</u>

Names: <u>Small yellow circle, small blue triangle, large yellow circle, large red rectangle, small red triangle, large red square</u>

1d. Number: <u>7</u>

Names: <u>Small blue triangle, large red circle, small blue rectangle, small yellow circle, large red rectangle, small yellow triangle, large blue circle</u>

2a.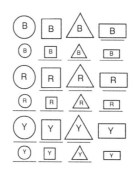

2b.

3a.

3b.

3c. Answers may vary.

3d. Answers may vary.

3e. Answers may vary.

3f. Answers may vary.

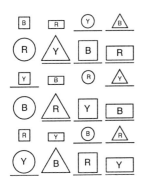

3g. Answers may vary.

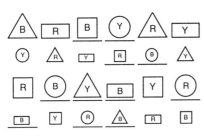

3h. Answers may vary.

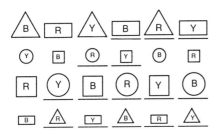

Matrices
Level 2—Assessments

1. Number: <u>5</u>

    Names: <u>Small blue rectangle</u>, <u>small yellow</u>
    <u>triangle</u>, <u>small red square</u>, <u>large yellow</u>
    <u>square, small red triangle</u>

2.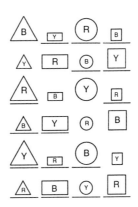

3a. Answers may vary.

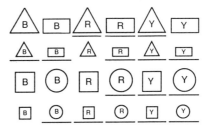

3b. Answers may vary.

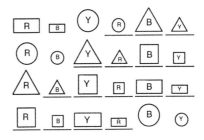

3c. Answers may vary.

3d.

Matrices
Level 3—Activities

1a. Number: <u>6</u>

    Names: <u>Small red hexagon</u>, <u>small yellow</u>

square, large yellow rectangle, large yellow circle, large red triangle, small yellow triangle

1b. Number: 7

Names: Large blue hexagon, small blue circle, large blue rectangle, small red triangle, small yellow rectangle, large yellow square, large yellow hexagon

1c. Number: 8

Names: Small red triangle, large yellow triangle, large red hexagon, small yellow rectangle, small red rectangle, small yellow square, large yellow square, small yellow circle

1d. Number: 9

Names: Large blue circle, small yellow triangle, small red triangle, small red hexagon, large yellow rectangle, large blue square, small yellow square, large blue triangle, small yellow circle

2a.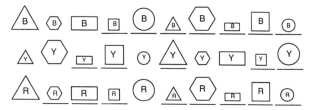

2b.

3a. Answers may vary.

3b. Answers may vary.

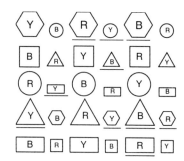

3c. Answers may vary.

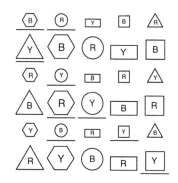

3d.

3e.

3f. Answers may vary.

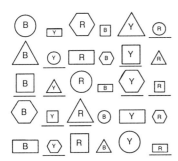

3g. Answers may vary.

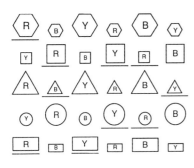

3h. Answers may vary.

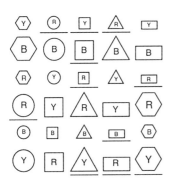

Matrices
Level 3—Assessments

1.   Number: <u>8</u>

    Names: <u>Large blue circle</u>, <u>large blue triangle</u>, <u>large yellow rectangle</u>, <u>large red rectangle</u>, <u>small yellow hexagon</u>, <u>small yellow square</u>, <u>small yellow triangle</u>, <u>small yellow rectangle</u>

2.

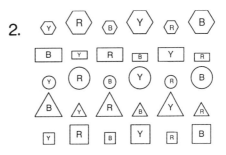

3a. Answers may vary.

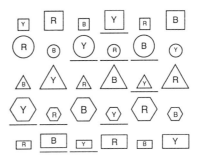

3b. Answers may vary.

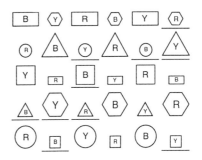

3c. Answers may vary.

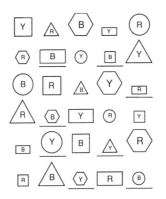

3d. Answers may vary.

TRAINS

Trains
Level 1—Activities

In some cases, there will be more than one possible answer.

1.

2.

3.

4.

5.

6.

Trains
Level 1—Assessments

1.

2.

3.

4.

5.

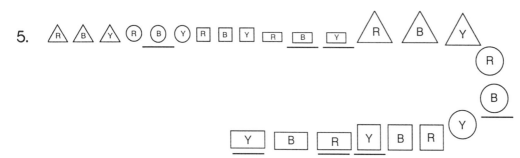

© 1998 Critical Thinking Books & Software • www.criticalthinking.com • 800-458-4849

Trains
Level 2—Activities

1.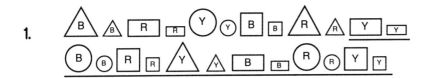

2. Answers may vary.

   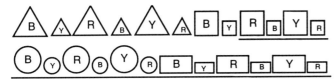

3.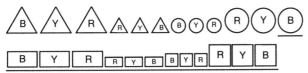

4.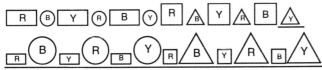

5.

6.

7.

8. Answers may vary.

9. Answers may vary.

10.

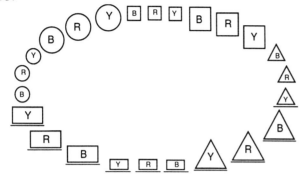

11.

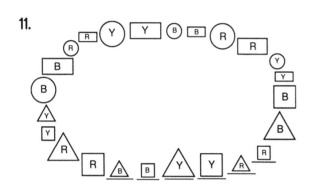

12.

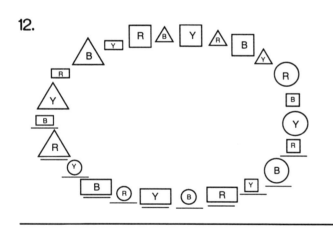

13.

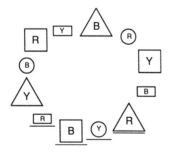

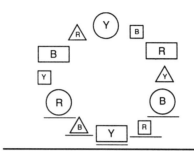

14.

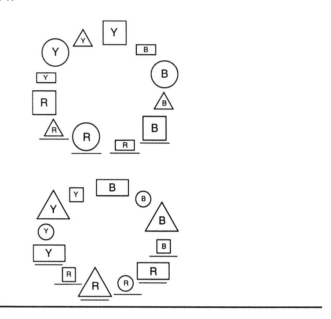

Trains
Level 2—Assessments

1.

2.

3.

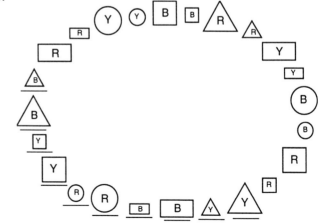

4.

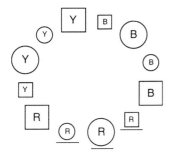

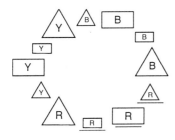

5.

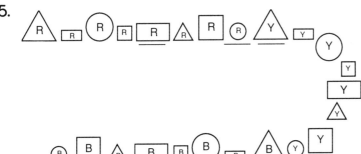

6.

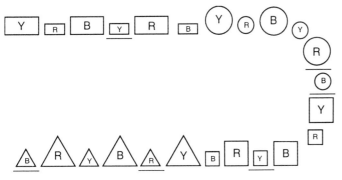

Trains
Level 3—Activities

1.

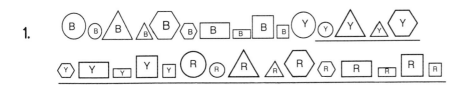

2.

3.

4.

5.

6.

7.

8.

9.

10.

11.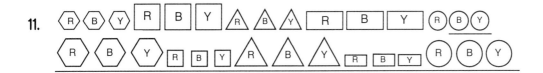

12.

13. Y R B B R Y Y R B B R Y Y R B
    B R Y Y R B B R Y Y R B B R Y

14. B Y B B Y B Y B Y R B R B R
    B R B R B Y R Y R Y R Y R Y R

15. B B B B B Y Y Y Y Y R R R R R
    B B B B B Y Y Y Y Y R R R R R

16.

17.

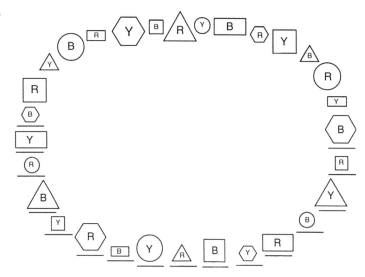

18.

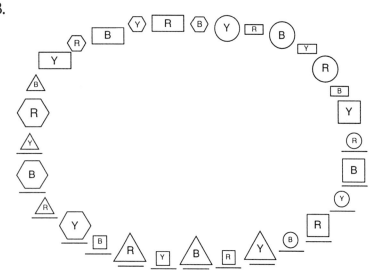

19.

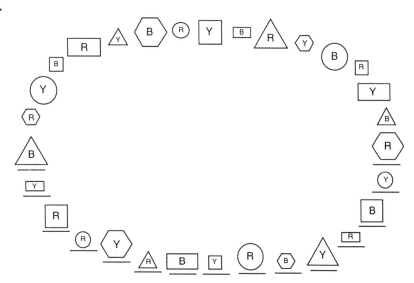

© 1998 Critical Thinking Books & Software • www.criticalthinking.com • 800-458-4849

20.

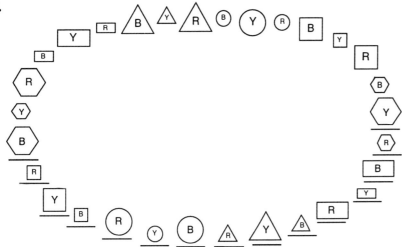

Trains
Level 3—Assessments

1. Answers may vary.

2.

3. Answers may vary.

4.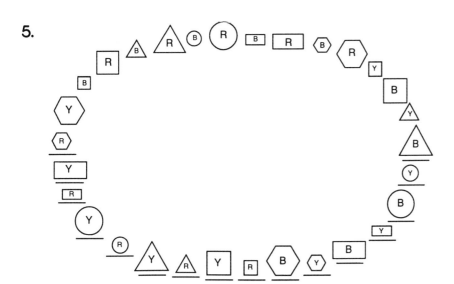

5.

6.

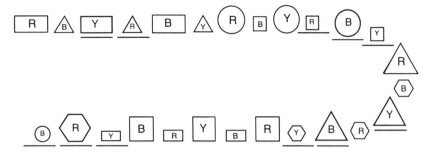

7.

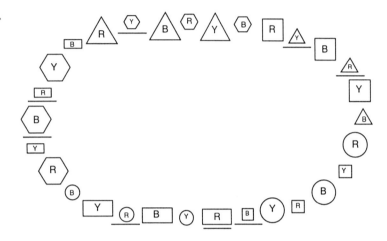

RINGS

Rings
Level 1—Activities

1. Any 3 yellow blocks inside
2. Any 4 square blocks inside
3. Any 5 small blocks inside
4. Any 6 red blocks inside
5. All 6 rectangles inside
6. All 12 large blocks inside
7. Any 3 non-square blocks outside
8. Any 4 non-yellow blocks outside
9. Any 5 small blocks outside
10. All 18 non-circle blocks outside
11. Any 3 blue blocks inside, any 3 non-blue blocks outside
12. Any 4 small blocks inside, any 4 large blocks outside
13. Any 5 triangles inside, any 5 non-triangles outside
14. All 8 yellow blocks inside, all 16 non-yellow blocks outside
15a. Red
15b. Circle
15c. Small

15d. Triangle
15e. Large
15f. Blue
16a. Large, Red
16b. Small, Rectangle
16c. Large, Blue, Circle
17a. Small non-square block or large square block
17b. Red non-triangle block or non-red triangle block
17c. Small blue block or large non-blue block

Rings
Level 1—Assessments

1. Any 3 squares inside
2. Any 3 non-yellow blocks outside
3. Any 3 small blocks inside, any 3 non-small blocks outside
4. Triangle
5. Blue, Square
6. Small yellow block or large non-yellow block

Rings
Level 2—Activities

1. Any 3 hexagons inside
2. Any 4 red blocks inside
3. Any 5 large blocks inside
4. All 6 triangles inside
5. All 10 yellow blocks inside
6. All 6 squares inside
7. Any 3 large blocks outside
8. Any 4 non-blue blocks outside
9. Any 5 non-circles outside
10. All 20 non-red blocks outside
11. Any 3 small blocks inside, any 3 large blocks outside
12. Any 4 rectangles inside, any 4 non-rectangles outside
13. Any 5 hexagons inside, any 5 non-hexagons outside
14. All 10 blue blocks inside, all 20 non-blue blocks outside
15a. Rectangle
15b. Yellow
15c. Large
15d. Small
15e. Hexagon

15f. Large
16a. Large, Hexagon
16b. Small, Yellow
16c. Small, Blue, Hexagon
17a. Small red block or large non-red block
17b. Large triangle or small non-triangle
17c. Blue non-hexagon or non-blue hexagon

Rings
Level 2—Assessments

1. Any 3 red blocks inside
2. Any 3 non-rectangles outside
3. Any 3 large blocks inside, any 3 small blocks outside
4. Hexagon
5. Rectangle, Yellow
6. Small non-hexagon or large hexagon

MYSTERY BLOCKS

Mystery Blocks
Level 1—Activities

1. Small red rectangle
2. Large yellow triangle
3. Small blue triangle
4. Large yellow rectangle
5. Small red square
6. Large blue triangle
7. Large yellow square
8. Large red rectangle

Mystery Blocks
Level 1—Assessments

1. Small blue rectangle
2. Small red triangle

Mystery Blocks
Level 2—Activities

1. Large blue triangle
2. Small blue hexagon
3. Small yellow rectangle
4. Large blue hexagon
5. Large red square
6. Large yellow circle
7. Small yellow hexagon
8. Small red triangle

Mystery Blocks
Level 2—Assessments

1. Small blue circle
2. Large yellow hexagon